PAUSES

Also by Lee Bennett Hopkins

I Can Read Books®
Surprises
More Surprises
Questions
Weather
Blast Off!

Picture Books
By Myself
Morning, Noon and Nighttime, Too
The Sky Is Full of Song
Best Friends
Good Books, Good Times!

Books for Middle Grades
Mama and Her Boys
Click, Rumble, Roar

Professional Reading
Pass the Poetry, Please!
Let Them Be Themselves

PAUSES

Autobiographical
Reflections
of 101 Creators of
Children's Books

LEE BENNETT HOPKINS

HarperCollins*Publishers*

Pauses
*Autobiographical Reflections
of 101 Creators of Children's Books*
Copyright © 1995 by Lee Bennett Hopkins
All rights reserved. No part of this book may be used or reproduced
in any manner whatsoever without written permission except in the
case of brief quotations embodied in critical articles and reviews.
Printed in the United States of America.
For information address HarperCollins Children's Books,
a division of HarperCollins Publishers,
10 East 53rd Street, New York, NY 10022.

Library of Congress Cataloging-in-Publication Data
Pauses : autobiographical reflections of 101 creators of children's books / by
Lee Bennett Hopkins.
        p.   cm.
    Includes index.
    ISBN 0-06-024748-7
    1. Children's literature, American—History and criticism—Theory, etc.
2. American literature—20th century—History and criticism—Theory, etc.
3. Authors, American—20th century—Interviews.   4. Illustrators—United
States—Interviews.   5. Children's literature—Illustrations.   6. Children's
literature—Authorship.   7. Illustrations of books.   I. Hopkins, Lee Bennett.
PS490.P38   1995   94-14641
810.9'9282—dc20   CIP
                                                                             AC

Typography by Steven M. Scott
1   2   3   4   5   6   7   8   9   10
❖
First Edition

To Charlotte S. Huck—

who caught me in her web.

LBH

Acknowledgments

Pauses would not be complete without my acknowledging a number of special individuals: Mary L. Allison, who once upon a time said, "Do it!"; Maurice Sendak, who helped pave the way; Misha Arenstein for his untiring patience; Charles J. Egita just because; Marlene Dietrich for inadvertently leading me to a format; Charlotte Zolotow, who acquired the initial manuscript; Sally Doherty for so much; Marilyn E. Marlow for forever being there for me; Ann Tobias, for her keen, insightful editorial guidance and who allowed me to pause to complete this volume. I am deeply indebted to all.

Contents

Author-Illustrators

Illustrators

Introduction

"Are authors real people, Mr. Hopkins?"
"Do authors live in regular houses or in publishing houses?"
"Were authors always authors?"

These questions, posed by students whom I taught early in my career as an elementary-school teacher, made me realize how curious children are about authors and illustrators who create works especially for them. I, too, began wondering about those names that appeared on the covers of books. Who were they? What were their childhood lives like? What inspired their ideas and ideologies? What motivated them to devote most of their lives to producing works for children? These questions led me on a many-year path, conducting interviews with creators of children's books.

Between the late 1960s and the early 1970s, I interviewed more than 150 authors and illustrators of children's books for various publishing projects I was engaged in. Over the decades that followed I continued to have hundreds more conversations with numerous authors and illustrators.

A question I am often asked is: "How *do* you select individuals to interview from such a myriad of people in the field of children's books?" I listen to comments by children, parents, teachers, librarians, and educators on every level. I am guided by the enthusiasm they have for particular books and their creators. I strive for balance, to include artists from various genres—from picture books to novels, nonfiction works to poetry. Of course, no single volume could include all the many individuals who contribute to the wide world of children's literature.

Many of the people featured in *Pauses* have received a bevy of awards, including the prestigious Newbery and Caldecott Medals. Many have not, yet their works continue to be read, loved, and shared from generation to generation, proving that wonderful, child-centered books can and do last because children themselves embrace them.

Pauses is a volume of reflective thoughts—pauses—expressed by children's book creators I have met, worked, and corresponded with. Each artist's reminiscences will spark young readers—the now and future teachers, librarians, parents, writers, and illustrators—to know the authors and artists included in this volume as human beings, to see them in a new light.

This book is divided into four sections: Authors, Author-Illustrators, Illustrators, and Poets; each section is arranged chronologically, based on the subjects' dates of birth. The earliest date herein, 1889, is the birth year of three all-time greats in the field of children's literature—James Daugherty, Marguerite de Angeli, and Elmer Hader; the latest is 1952, when Robin McKinley was born.

Each of our lives is filled with pauses—pauses between being born and growing up, reaching adulthood, and finding one's way in life to achieve, succeed—pauses between middle and old age—pauses even after death.

Pauses reflects the lives of 101 individuals who have chosen to use their talents to enrich children's lives.

Pause.

Enjoy *Pauses*.

Lee Bennett Hopkins
Scarborough, New York

PAUSES

Authors

It begins with a word or phrase . . .
—Natalie Babbitt

And the word or phrase is extended into sentences, paragraphs—into short or long picture books, nonfiction books, or novels. Words grow to create worlds that reflect children's lives—past and present—or take them to worlds they never thought possible. A word or phrase set down on paper eventually leads to a book that generations of readers will relish.

Marguerite de Angeli

Marguerite de Angeli was born on March 14, 1889, in Lapeer, Michigan. In 1902, when she was thirteen, she moved with her family to Philadelphia, Pennsylvania, where she lived until her death on June 16, 1987. Her first book, Ted and Nina Go to the Grocery Store, *appeared in 1935 (Westminster Press), followed by a series of titles featuring Ted and Nina. Her novel* The Door in the Wall *(1949) received the Newbery Medal, and another novel,* Black Fox of Lorne *(1956), is a Newbery Honor Book. Two books that she illustrated,* Yonie Wondernose *(1944) and* Book of Nursery and Mother Goose Rhymes *(1954; all Doubleday) are Caldecott Honor Books. She received the Regina Medal in 1968. In 1992 Doubleday established the Marguerite de Angeli Prize, an annual award for an outstanding work of fiction for seven- to ten-year-olds.*

My longing to write and illustrate goes back to childhood, but there were so many other things I wanted to do that it was pushed aside, partly because my father, who was very gifted himself in art, didn't encourage me. I think he was fearful that I might get into loose company! A thing I would never have done. My mother did encourage me, but as there wasn't much money, nothing was done about it.

Meantime, a neighbor heard me singing and offered me a position in the church choir. I went on from there, studying singing. At nineteen I was offered a part in *Samson and Delilah,* an opera by Oscar Hammerstein I. After one rehearsal and the prospect of going with the company to London, my parents persuaded me that by marrying the young man to whom I was engaged, I would lead a much happier and more satisfying life than that of an opera singer. I listened and never regretted it.

The need to draw and write kept popping up, but children did too. When the children numbered three, I met Maurice Bower, then a well-known illustrator, who gave me help and criticism. After a year of working on several subjects, I was given a story to do for Westminster Press. It just went on from there. After I spent fifteen years illustrating magazines and books, Helen Ferris, head of the Junior Literary Guild, suggested that I write the text as well for a book for six-year-olds. I did! *Ted and Nina Go to the Grocery Store* was based on the activities of two of my five children.

The title for *The Door in the Wall* came from a belief I passed along to my children: "When you come to a stone wall, if you look hard enough, you will find a door in it."

The writing and illustrating of a book in its early stages is a great joy. The characters become real and sometimes move around in a strange fashion—then comes the hard work of whipping it into final shape and putting on the finishing touches.

Winning the Newbery Medal was immensely exciting because it was the most important award up to that time. However, after I had been awarded what is considered to be the ultimate prize in writing for children, it was difficult to go on and do another book. Some time elapsed before I began another story for children.

I never had a favorite among my many books because each one meant a whole collection of new friends and new scenes. I hope that as time has passed I have improved in writing and illustrating. I still hear echoes from even my earliest books, especially *Thee, Hannah!* and *Yonie Wondernose* [both reissued by Doubleday in 1990], which deal with Pennsylvania Dutch families and their customs.

Elizabeth Coatsworth

Elizabeth Coatsworth was born on May 31, 1893, in Buffalo, New York. After she published three volumes of adult poetry, her first book for children, The Cat and the Captain, *appeared in 1927.* The Cat Who Went to Heaven *(1930; both Macmillan) received the Newbery Medal. Author of close to one hundred books for children, she was recipient of the 1975 Kerlan Award. She died in 1986 at her home at Chimney Farm in Nobleboro, Maine.*

I was born in Buffalo at the eastern end of Lake Erie, near the Niagara River. My family owned a grain elevator there, which stored grain brought in by the great freighters until it could be shipped by the Erie Canal and the Hudson River to New York City.

We traveled a good deal. Before I went to Vassar College, where I graduated with a bachelor of arts degree in 1915, I had spent eight months abroad as a little girl, gone to high school for two years in California, and spent a long Christmas holiday in Mexico in the old resplendent days before the revolution. After college I never went back to Buffalo to live, but was sometimes in California and sometimes in New England.

Nineteen nineteen was a wonderful year. The war to end war, as we thought at that time, had been fought and won. Everywhere there were new beginnings. One of these was the creation by the Macmillan Company of the first separate department of children's books, to which they invited Louise Seaman as editor. Louise and I had been friends at Vassar, and after college she taught for a few years in New Haven, Connecticut. She was well read, discriminating, and decisive. As an editor she listened to a writer's ideas, asked intelligent questions, and then challenged one to put the ideas into form. When a manuscript was finished, Louise read it and either approved the result or put the author on his mettle to do a better book.

My own interest was in poetry and playwriting. But one day, while I was commenting on one of the books Louise had published, she challenged me, "Write a better one then." And I did! I wrote *The Cat and the Captain*, writing one small chapter each night. And I have been writing children's books ever since.

In 1916 and 1917 my mother, sister, and I spent a month in Kyoto, Japan. In one of the old temples we were shown a picture of the death of the Buddha, which included one of the attendant animals, a cat. "This is very unusual," said the monk guide. "The cat is usually not shown because of its lack of humility." Later we were in Java and visited the old Buddhist temples. Carved letters included the animal incarnations of the

Buddha. These things lay unnoticed in my mind for ten years, until the winter before my marriage to Henry Beston. I was staying in California when they began to take form. In a week I had written *The Cat Who Went to Heaven*, illustrated it myself, and typed it. My drawings, never used, were the basis for Lynd Ward's final artwork.

I love to write, but like any other craft, there are hours of correcting, polishing, and rewriting that a writer must be ready to put in, as well as the wonderful hours of writing, when the pen seems to be running away with the story. I have no theories about writing children's books except that any book should in some way sharpen the reader's appetite for living, whether the reader be seven or seventy. A writer is an amalgam of all ages. I recall vividly what it is to be twenty-five or five. You know because you were.

Lois Lenski

Lois Lenski was born on October 14, 1893, in Springfield, Ohio, the fourth of five children. Her childhood and early youth were spent in Anna, Ohio, a small farming town where her father was a Lutheran minister. After receiving a B.S. degree in education from Ohio State University in 1915, she studied at the Art Students League in New York City. In 1920 she went to England to further her art studies at the Westminster School of Arts in London. During her lifetime she wrote and illustrated scores of books for children. Two of her books, Phebe Fairchild: Her book *(Stokes, 1936) and* Indian Captive: The Story of Mary

Jemison *(Lippincott, 1941; reissued by Harper, 1994), are Newbery Honor Books. She received the Newbery Medal for* Strawberry Girl *(Lippincott, 1945). In addition to a number of other awards, she received both the Regina Medal and the University of Southern Mississippi Medallion in 1969. She died on September 11, 1974, in Tarpon Springs, Florida.*

While studying in London, I did my first illustrations for children's books. I illustrated *The Golden Age* by Kenneth Grahame and *The Green-Faced Toad* by Vera B. Birch [both John Lane, 1921]. When I returned to the United States, I found that children's book publishing was beginning to develop at a rapid pace. In 1928 *A Little Girl of 1900* [Stokes] was published, a story drawn directly from my own childhood experiences.

My travels have taken me to all parts of the country—the mountains of North Carolina, the oil fields of Oklahoma, and the cornfields of Iowa. I have tried to describe how people live in different places. Actual people, seen and known in different regions, become my main characters. Each time I draw a character, I hold in my memory the image of the real person I saw who inspired it. I cannot write a story if I cannot visualize both the characters and the setting.

One can describe only the outward things: Days spent talking to children and listening—always listening; visiting their schools, their homes; getting to know their parents and earning their confidence; eating at the kitchen table in the heart of the family.

To write of real children means a close rapport with them, a positive identification with them. I must *be* that child in spirit for many months while the work is in progress. I eat, sleep, speak, and act as the child acts. He becomes more real to me than members of my own family whom I am seeing daily, because I have entered his mind and thought. I think and feel as he thinks and feels. He comes alive under my pencil.

Even in a picture book for the preschool child, I must somehow catch up the essence of the small child's world, forget my adult world and way of thinking, become a child at heart, live with him, his simple doings and activity, listen to his every word with respect, and try to interpret all he does. To the very young child, a drawing is not a picture on paper, it is a real happening. The author-artist must sense this, and draw pictures that have the breath of life in them.

Writing and drawing each take a turn; each reinforces the other. My stories are tried out on children of the age the book is intended for. If a drawing is not clear or a word is unfamiliar, the child will let you know. I respect a child's thinking and direct appraisal—his spontaneous reaction to a story or pictures—far more highly than my own adult notions.

Carol Ryrie Brink

Carol Ryrie Brink was born on December 28, 1895, in Moscow, Idaho. Her first book for children, Anything Can Happen on the River, *appeared in 1934. Her second book,* Caddie Woodlawn

(1935; both Macmillan), received the Newbery Medal and is still popular with readers today. The author went on to write many more books for children and was the recipient of the 1978 Kerlan Award. Carol Ryrie Brink died on August 15, 1981, in La Jolla, California.

I grew up in Moscow, a small university town in a region of rolling wheat fields and blue mountains. I lost my father when I was five, my mother when I was eight, and I went to live with a very wonderful grandmother and a loving and indulgent aunt. Much of my childhood was lonely, but it was not unhappy—just enough unhappiness to make me think and appreciate.

Because I was lonely, I learned a most valuable thing—how to make my own amusements by reading, writing, drawing, making things with my hands, and spending many happy hours on horseback. I always had animal friends—dogs, cats, and pet chickens. My grandmother and aunt were both great storytellers, and I lived vicariously the exciting childhood that my grandmother had lived on the Wisconsin frontier. Her stories were one of the delights of my earlier years.

I had always wanted to write books, and at first I wrote and published some poetry. I have written poetry all my life, but after I began writing prose, I no longer tried to publish the poems. When my two children, David and Nora, were small, they brought home Sunday-school papers for me to read aloud. As I read the stories, I said to myself, "If I can't do better than that, it is too bad." So I sent my first children's stories to Sunday-school papers, and they were kindly received by friendly editors. I learned more in this humble field than I ever learned from creative-writing courses in college.

Had I not been an orphan, *Caddie Woodlawn* might never have been written, since the episodes of my grandmother's life were the natural background for the book. *Caddie* is Grandmother's story, and I loved hearing it as a child. I find that children are always delighted to know that the story is true. *Caddie* has made me so many friends all over the world that I must always be grateful to the book—to her—to Gram.

Carolyn Haywood

Carolyn Haywood, born on January 3, 1898, in Philadelphia, Pennsylvania, grew up in Germantown, a nearby suburb. Her first book, B Is for Betsy *(Harcourt, 1939), was followed by many titles in the Betsy series. Her last book,* Eddie's Friend, Boodles *(Morrow, 1990), was published posthumously. She died January 11, 1990, in Philadelphia.*

As a young girl I spent most of my spare time drawing and painting, with the ambition of becoming an artist. After graduating from the Philadelphia High School for Girls and the Philadelphia Normal School, I taught for a year. At the end of the year I was granted a scholarship to study art at the Pittsburgh Academy of Fine Arts. I studied there for three years; it was here that I won a Cresson European Scholarship. I began my career as a portrait painter specializing in children.

In the 1930s I decided to try my hand at writing and illustrating a children's book. I planned a picture book with little text, but Elizabeth Hamilton, an editor at Harcourt, suggested that I write about American children and the things that interest them. *B Is for Betsy* evolved from that suggestion and my writing career for children was launched.

I derive experiences from various sources. I just listen to everything people tell me, and in that way ideas come to me. Many of my own experiences while a child have found their way into my books. I travel fairly widely and make notes and sketches. Travel has given me background material for a number of books.

Of all delightful features about make-believe children, the most convenient one is that their author can control not only their growing up but their growing down. The world of books is indeed an *Alice in Wonderland* world where there are bottles marked "Drink me" and cakes marked "Eat me" with the inevitable Alice results.

Scott O'Dell

Scott O'Dell, a descendant of Sir Walter Scott, was born on May 23, 1898, in Los Angeles, California. After he worked in motion pictures, wrote for newspapers and magazines, and created several adult books, his first novel for children, Island of the Blue Dolphins *(1960), received the Newbery Medal and was made into a film. Three of his twenty-five novels are Newbery Honor Books:* The King's Fifth *(1966),* The Black Pearl *(1967), and* Sing Down the Moon *(1970). The many awards he received include the 1972 Hans Christian Andersen Medal, the 1976 University of Southern Mississippi Medallion, and the 1978 Regina Medal. In 1981 he founded the Scott O'Dell Award for Historical Fiction to encourage writers of this genre. He died on October 15, 1989, in Waccubuc, New York. His last novel,* Thunder Rolling in the Mountains, *left unfinished at the time of his death, was completed by his wife, Elizabeth Hall, and published in 1992 (all Houghton).*

Los Angeles was a frontier town when I was born there around the turn of the century. It had more horses than automobiles, more jackrabbits than people. The very first sound I remember was a wildcat scratching on the roof as I lay in bed.

My father was a railroad man, so we moved a lot. There was San Pedro, which is a part of Los Angeles. And Rattlesnake Island, across the bay from San Pedro, where we lived in a house on stilts and the waves came up and washed under us every day. And sailing ships went by. That is why, I suppose, the feel of the frontier and the sound of the sea are in my books. This also explains why many of the people I have written about are Indians, Spaniards, and Chicanos.

Grammar school and high school fascinated me. But not college—not Occidental nor Stanford nor the University of Wisconsin. By this time I had my heart set upon writing. However, most of the courses I was forced to take to graduate had little to do with learning to write. So I forgot graduation and took only the courses I wanted—psychology, philosophy, history, and English.

Island of the Blue Dolphins was based on the true story of a girl who was left upon an island near the coast of Southern California and lived there alone for eighteen years. The novel was written without any thought of who might read it. In fact, I didn't know what young people were reading and I didn't consider it a children's book. I sent the story to my agents. They sent it back by return mail, saying that if I was serious about the story I should change the main character from a girl to a boy because girls were only interested in romance and such. This seemed silly to me. So I went to Houghton and gave the manuscript to my editor, who accepted it the next day.

In 1961, I spent part of the summer in Navaho country, where the states of Arizona and New Mexico, Colorado, and Utah meet. *Sing Down the Moon*, the story of Bright Morning and her flock of sheep, is the result of those days among the Navahos. I think of it as a modest tribute not only to this Indian girl but also to the courage of the human spirit.

Childhood is very important. I hope that somewhere in each of my books there is something personal that young people will remember. Of all the audiences, children are the finest.

E. B. White

E. B. White was born on July 11, 1899, in Mount Vernon, New York, the last of six children. In 1921, upon his graduation from Cornell University, he moved to New York City. He joined the staff of The New Yorker *magazine in 1926 and continued to write for it throughout his life. His first book,* The Lady Is Cold, *written for an adult audience, appeared in 1929. In 1945 he published the first of his three books for children,* Stuart Little, *followed by* Charlotte's Web *(1952), a Newbery Honor Book, and* The Trumpet of the Swan *(1970; all Harper). His many honors include the 1963 Presidential Medal of Freedom and the 1970 Laura Ingalls Wilder Award. He died on October 1, 1985, at his home in North Brooklin, Maine.*

Many years ago I went to bed one night in a railway sleeping car, and during the night I dreamed about a tiny boy who acted rather like a mouse. That's how the story of Stuart Little got started. It took about twelve years to do Stuart, but most of the time I did not think I was writing a book. I was busy with other matters.

I like animals and my barn is a very pleasant place to be, at all hours. One day when I was on my way to feed the pig, I began feeling sorry for the pig because, like most pigs, he was doomed to die. This made me sad. So I started thinking of ways to save a pig's life. I had been watching a big gray spider at her work and was impressed by how clever she was at weaving. Gradually I worked the spider into *Charlotte's Web*, a story of friendship and salvation on a farm.

Before attempting the book, I studied spiders and boned up on them. I watched Charlotte at work, here on my place, and I also read books about the life of spiders, to inform myself about their habits, their capabilities, their temperament. Having finished the book, I was dissatisfied with it, so instead of submitting it to my publisher, I laid it aside for a while, then rewrote it introducing Fern and other characters. This took a year, but it was a year well spent. Three years after I started writing *Charlotte's Web*, it was published. (I am not a fast worker, as you can see.)

Sometimes I'm asked how old I was when I started to write, and what made me want to write. I started early—as soon as I could spell. In fact, I can't remember any time in my life when I wasn't busy writing. I don't know what caused me to do it, or why I enjoyed it, but I think children often find pleasure and satisfaction in trying to set their thoughts down on paper, either in words or in pictures. I was no good at drawing, so I used words instead. As I grew older, I found that writing can be a way of earning a living.

My stories are imaginary tales, containing fantastic characters and events. In *real* life, a family doesn't have a child who looks like a mouse; in *real* life, a spider doesn't spin words in her web. In *real* life, a swan doesn't blow a trumpet. But real life is only one kind of life—there is also the life of the imagination. And although my stories are imaginary, I like to think that there is some truth in them, too—truth about the way people and animals feel and think and act.

I don't know how or when the idea for *Trumpet of the Swan* occurred to me. I guess I must have wondered what it would be like to be a Trumpeter Swan and not be able to make any noise.

There is a difference between writing for children and adults. I am lucky, though, as I seldom seem to have my audience in mind when I am at work. It is as though they didn't exist.

Children are the most attentive, curious, eager, observant, sensitive, quick, and generally congenial readers on earth. They accept, almost without question, anything you present them with, as long as it is presented honestly, fearlessly, and clearly.

My own vocabulary is small, compared to most writers, and I tend to use the short words. So it's no problem for me to write for children. We have a lot in common.

Jean Lee Latham

Jean Lee Latham was born on April 19, 1902, in Buckhannon, West Virginia, and began writing plays while she was in high school. In 1930, after working in a variety of teaching roles, she became the editor of the Dramatic Publishing Company in Chicago, Illinois. Her first book for children, The Story of Eli Whitney *(Aladdin, 1953), appeared eighteen years after her first adult book,* Do's and Don'ts of Drama: 555 Pointers for Beginning Actors and Directors *(Dramatic Publishing Company, 1935).* Carry On, Mr. Bowditch *(Houghton, 1955) received the Newbery Medal. She lives in Coral Gables, Florida.*

Growing up in Buckhannon, I spent a lot of happy years at the three R's—readin', ritin', and runnin' around! For years I lived just across from a lovely bit of unpruned forest. We had swings, trapezes, log and tree houses. The only things I did indoors, sometimes, were read, write poetry, and tell stories to my younger brothers and their pals. So I do what comes naturally when I write for children—especially for boys.

From 1928 to 1959, I wrote stage and radio plays. One day a man showed me a model of the first cotton gin and said, "I wonder what would have happened if Eli Whitney had been a lawyer, as he started out to be." Since I'm a dramatist at heart, that was enough to start me, tally-ho, on his trail. I always look for the suspense in a man's life. If there's not enough suspense, the man's just not my cup of tea.

Nathaniel Bowditch was a self-taught man who became one of the leading mathematicians in the United States. I got the inspiration to do *Carry On, Mr. Bowditch* after I had read one single paragraph in Bowditch's book on navigation, *The American Practical Navigator,* a work that is still used by sailors the world over.

I thought about the book in a series of *that*s: That the undersized son of a drunkard had to stop school when he was ten. That when he was twelve, he was given six weeks of training in bookkeeping and then was apprenticed to a ship chandlery and could not leave the premises by night or day without permission, until he was twenty-one years old. That by the time he was thirty, he had conceived of a new method of nautical calculations and had written the book that is still the sailor's Bible. That he could read Latin, French, and other languages. That he was the outstanding mathematician in the United States and was awarded a master's degree from Harvard: Well, there just *had* to be a story *there*, no? There was, and I wanted to tell it— even though I knew absolutely nothing about anything I'd have to know to do it!

When I read the letter telling me I had won the Newbery Award, I looked up "Newbery" in the encyclopedia, called my sister to borrow some winter clothes for a trek to New York City for the award ceremony, then returned home and got back to my writing.

Walter Farley

Walter Farley, born on June 26, 1902, in Syracuse, New York, is known throughout the world for his adventurous tales about horses. Two of the twenty novels in the Black Stallion series, The Black Stallion *(1941) and* The Black Stallion Returns *(1945), were made into successful films.* The Young Black Stallion *(1989; all Random House), coauthored with his eldest son, Steven*

Farley, was published posthumously. Walter Farley lived in Venice, Florida, and on a farm near Earlsville, Pennsylvania, and died on October 17, 1989.

I lived in midtown Manhattan at the Hotel Roosevelt, where my father worked as an assistant manager. I commuted by subway to Erasmus Hall High School in Brooklyn, because the school had a good track team. I loved New York City. There were plenty of horses—in Central Park, Squadron A with its indoor polo, Long Island, Connecticut, and Westchester trails, and the racetracks at Belmont, Jamaica, and Aqueduct, where I spent many, many days. Later I moved to Flushing, Queens, where several of my friends had horses stabled in lots now occupied by apartment buildings. And it was there I set the locale for *The Black Stallion* as I rode on trails through Kissena Park and along the Long Island Expressway.

At fourteen, fifteen, and sixteen, I enjoyed writing stories on the typewriter, any kind of story at all. I read a great deal, but there were few books about horses—at least only a couple that I knew of. There was Anna Sewell's *Black Beauty* and Will James's *Smoky, the Cow Horse*, but these were not enough to satisfy me; I honestly thought, even at that age, about the thousands of horse lovers like me who wanted more books about horses. So I had fun writing *The Black Stallion* for them and for myself. I remember devoting two and three nights a week writing it while attending Erasmus. I continued writing the book as a student at Mercersburg Academy in Pennsylvania; it was published while I was an undergraduate at Columbia

University in New York City. I used the advance on the book to go traveling!

I have no occupation other than writing. The only income I've ever had has come from writing books. I do raise racehorses and Arabians occasionally and sell them, but there's really little money in it. Writing for me is fun. All my books are completely different from one another; otherwise I could never have stayed with the same characters who are used as springboards into whatever it is I want to write about. Kids know how different my books are; most adults don't. I've written fantasy and science fiction. *The Black Stallion's Ghost* [Random House, 1969] is a horror story of the supernatural; *Man o' War* [Random House, 1962], the story of one of America's mightiest Thoroughbred racing horses, is a fictional biography—authentic but seen through the eyes of a fictitious stableboy.

Children's letters have always been important to me. I don't really know how many hundreds of thousands of letters I've received over the years, but I've read them all. How different are kids in their love for horses now than they were in the 1940s? I think little. Many kids would rather ride on the back of a horse at twenty to twenty-five miles per hour than pilot a spaceship to the moon!

Harold Keith

Harold Keith, born on April 8, 1903, in Lambert, Oklahoma Territory, began his career as a seventh-grade teacher in the Amroita Oklahoma Consolidated School System in the early 1920s. After working as a reporter on the Hutchinson, Kansas, newspaper from 1930 to 1969, he was the sports publicity director at the University of Oklahoma in Norman. In 1936 his first book for children, Boy's Life of Will Rogers, *appeared.* Rifles for Watie *(1957; both Crowell) received the Newbery Medal, and in 1993 he donated the Medal to the Norman, Oklahoma, Public Library, where it is on permanent display.*

We lived in Watonga, Oklahoma, a smallish county seat that had a population of 1,500. My father owned the ice house and ice-cream plant. In those distant days at Watonga there was no radio, television, or paved roads. In spite of the town's isolation, its inhabitants knew how to have fun. Town baseball was the annual summer craze. Enthusiasm was carried over into October. I recall that during the 1919 World Series between Chicago and Cincinnati, Hooper's corner drugstore was jammed with people watching my high school pal chalk up the score by innings. It was my job to run back and forth to the Rock Island railroad station, where the agent obligingly bootlegged this sketchy information off the depot wire. It was like a message on the bush telegraph.

I probably decided to write for children because I had been doing it early in life. At fourteen I began writing fiction for a weekly magazine, *Lone Scout*. Boys from all over the nation wrote the entire magazine and also did the artwork. The Lone Scout organization paralleled the Boy Scouts but was designed for farm and small-town kids. We weren't paid for our work. Later I wrote short stories about sports for *The American Boy*. I enjoyed it; the magazine's standards were high, and we got paid!

My first book, *Boy's Life of Will Rogers*, came about when Will Rogers, an Oklahoman, died in 1935 in an Alaskan plane crash. Crowell, the publishers, sought an author to write a biography of him. They wanted an Oklahoman. The editor of *The American Boy* suggested me.

Rifles for Watie was my sixth book. As a history student at the university back in the 1920s, I became interested in the Cherokee Indians living in eastern Oklahoma and how superior their culture, wealth, and education were to that of the whites living around them.

Researching *Boy's Life of Will Rogers* had brought me in contact with Clem Rogers, Will's father, who was a Cherokee politician and had been a captain in General Stand Watie's Cherokee cavalry during the Civil War. I thought him a more interesting man than Will Rogers. So for my master's thesis in history I chose the subject "Clem Rogers and His Influence on Oklahoma History."

From all this I felt *Rifles for Watie* developing. During the summers of 1939 and 1940, I obtained a list from the state capital of all the rebel Civil War veterans still living in Oklahoma and called on them; there were about twenty. I interviewed each, writing down their personal memories; the facts filled three notebooks. I have always enjoyed interviewing old people. You get a great deal of color, personality, and characterization. I haunted the various state historical societies, scanning letters and diaries of Union Civil War soldiers. I let all this information lie dormant until after I'd taken a few courses in the University of Oklahoma's professional writing school. *Rifles* . . . was my first book thereafter.

Winning the Newbery Medal changed my life in that I've become a prolific writer of letters. I've received hundreds of letters from youngsters about this book, and I've answered every one.

I develop ideas for books from research. When I find a field I like, I research it heavily. I revise six or seven times. Sometimes I check the manuscript with children. When I'm at work on a book, I become very enthusiastic about it and think it's going to be the best book I ever wrote. The writing is great fun. No matter how tired I am, I dislike stopping. I can't wait to resume the following morning.

Elizabeth Borten de Treviño

Elizabeth Borten de Treviño was born on September 2, 1904, in Bakersfield, California. In 1934, while on a newspaper assignment in Mexico, she met Luis Treviño Gomez, whom she married a year later, and settled in Mexico, where she still lives. Her novel I, Juan de Pareja *(Farrar, 1965) received the Newbery Medal.*

I had an unusually happy childhood. My father, a lawyer, always took us on weekend picnics; I spent my summers with a beloved grandmother at Monterey on the coast. Our family was close; we read together in the winter in front of the fireplace, and my mother and grandmother taught my sister and me how to sew, knit, crochet, and tat.

I studied English literature in high school and at Stanford University, but I have written since I was eight years old. I always had severe but helpful critics in my parents and teachers. My work as a reporter for the *Boston Herald*, a job I held for seven years, provided excellent training. I have always loved books and stories, and so far as I can determine, the story is the thing in all writing for children.

I generally get story ideas from some true event or moment in history that fires my imagination. All of my books contain a little kernel of truth, something that really happened. Each of my stories tries to show some phase of love, that powerful emotion that makes the world go round.

It was my son, Luis, who, while studying painting, learned the true story of Juan de Pareja and told it to me. I loved the story, and when I saw a reproduction of the portrait Velázquez painted of Juan, I was determined to write about him, for his face seemed to me to be that of a dignified, noble, and proud person whose story should be told.

I looked for information in many books—all in Spanish, and they were at variance on many points. But the main outline was clear: a slave had secretly taught himself to paint, had confessed this to his master, and had been freed and elevated to the position of "assistant" by Velázquez. The two men started out as master and slave, continued through life as companions, and ended as equals and friends.

Winning the Newbery Award reaffirmed for me a deep sense of professional responsibility.

Elizabeth Yates

Elizabeth Yates was born on December 6, 1905, in Buffalo, New York. From 1926 to 1929, she worked in New York doing various types of writing—book reviews, articles, and stories. After marrying William McGreal, a businessman, she moved to London, England, where her first book for children, High Holiday *(Black, 1938), was published. Returning to the United States in the late 1930s, she continued to write books for adults and children.* Mountain Born *(Coward, 1943) is a Newbery Honor Book; she received the Newbery Medal for* Amos Fortune, Free Man *(Aladdin, 1950; reprinted by Dutton in 1958). She lives in Peterborough, New Hampshire.*

The most memorable days of my childhood years were the long summers spent on my father's farm in the rich, rolling country south of Buffalo. I often would go off on my horse for a day at a time rambling through the countryside, a sandwich in my pocket and the knowledge that any fresh-running stream would give us both a cool drink. I was never lonely, for there was the horse to talk with, and in my head I was writing stories. On the next rainy day I'd climb the ladder to an unused pigeon loft, my own secret place, and there I wrote down in a series of copybooks all that I had been thinking about.

It was after I had written a number of books, both fiction and nonfiction, for children and adults, that on a summer evening I was on my way to attend the Amos Fortune Lecture Series in the little town of Jaffrey Center, about seven miles from my home in Peterborough. Before attending the lecture, I went to the churchyard on the hilltop to see Amos Fortune's grave. Beside it stood one for his wife, Violet. I read the inscriptions of both markers:

> *Sacred to the memory of AMOS FORTUNE who was born free in Africa. A slave in America he purchased liberty, professed Christianity, lived reputably, and died hopefully, Nov. 17, 1801, Aet. 91*

> *Sacred to the memory of VIOLET by sale the slave of Amos Fortune, by marriage his wife, by her fidelity his friend and solace, she died his widow, Sept. 13, 1802, Aet. 73*

I stood by the stones in the cemetery in Jaffrey and I wanted to know more. I did research on his life for one year, the life of a man who was once an African prince who became a slave in Boston, a man who at the age of sixty bought his freedom and helped others to do the same.

I studied his papers, his will, and African slave trading records and saw his home and the personal items that had been left. After my notes had grown over an inch thick, I began writing the story.

Receiving the Newbery Medal was a total surprise. My feeling always has been that it went to Amos more than to me, and for this I am glad.

My work is about equally divided between fiction and biography for adults and books for children. I never really decided to write for children. It simply is that some stories seem to be the sort of ones that are tellable for girls and boys.

Research for a book often requires long hours in libraries, sometimes travel and interviews. My first draft is done in longhand with sharp pencils on yellow legal pads. The revision is my favorite stage of work—when words are in hand and the whole can be brought to my idea of perfection; then the finished copy is typed and goes off to the publisher. I never had any type of formal training in writing.

I have no favorites among the many different types of books I have written. I love them all, and each one represented something I very much wanted to express. The most recent, like the youngest child, is the nearest to me and the one I feel most tender about.

Meindert DeJong

Meindert DeJong, born on March 4, 1906, in Weirom in the Netherlands, came to the United States in 1914 at the age of eight. He won numerous national and international awards for his children's books. In 1962 he became the first American author to win the Hans Christian Andersen Award; he was also the recipient of the 1972 Regina Medal. Hurry Home Candy *(1953),* Shadrach *(1953),* The House of Sixty Fathers *(1956), and* Along Came a Dog *(1958), all illustrated by Maurice*

Sendak, are Newbery Honor Books. He received the Newbery Medal for The Wheel on the School *(1954; all Harper), also illustrated by Maurice Sendak. He died on July 16, 1991, in Allegen, Michigan.*

M y parents, descendants from French Huguenot families, fled to Friesland during the persecution of the Protestant religion. When I was eight years old, we came to the United States and settled in Grand Rapids, Michigan. My three brothers and I spent our first few days here in the new country searching for a dike!

I was educated at local religious schools maintained by Dutch Calvinists. Father was busy earning a living, Mother was so homesick that she refused to learn English, and school life was unhappy because of language problems. Add this to a loss of beloved grandparents, and it added up to a lonely childhood.

After I graduated from John Calvin College in Michigan, where I majored in English, we were smack in the middle of the Depression. I went to work on a farm my father had bought when his business failed. In the evenings, after a sixteen-hour workday, I wrote short stories for magazines that kept going out of business before they could pay me. I sold eggs to the Grand Rapids Public Library, and when the children's librarian there heard of my tales of a pet goose and a duck, she insisted that I write out the story. This led to my first book, *The Big Goose and the Little White Duck*, published in 1938; it was reissued in 1963, with new illustrations by Nancy Elkholm Burkert [Harper].

I never decided to write for children. A librarian, a goose, and a duck decided it for me. I owned the goose and duck; they were wonderful pets.

During World War II, I spent three years in Chungking, China, in the little village of Peishiyi, as official historian for [American General Claire Lee] Chennault's 14th Air Force, an experience on which *The House of Sixty Fathers* is based. The Chinese were fascinated by my blond hair and persistently wanted to feel it, though women often ran from me in fright. Because of my hair color, I was treated in some villages as one of the venerable old men and was invited to sip tea with them. Possibly, *The House of Sixty Fathers* is my favorite book, since the experience was real to me.

For pride, security, and self-belief, the most meaningful award I have received is the Newbery Medal. But even more important than that was receiving the Aurienne Award, given for books that help develop humane attitudes toward animals. This was given to me in warmth and for animal love. And it required no speech!

Eleanor Estes

Eleanor Estes was born on May 9, 1906, in West Haven, Connecticut. After finishing high school, she worked in the children's department of the New Haven Free Public Library. Moving to New York City, she worked in various children's departments of the

New York Public Library system until 1940. Her first book, The Moffats, *was published in 1941. Her Newbery Honor Books include* The Middle Moffat *(1942),* Rufus M. *(1943), and* The Hundred Dresses *(1944), all illustrated by Louis Slobodkin.* Ginger Pye *(1951; all Harcourt), which she wrote and illustrated, received the Newbery Medal. She died in 1988.*

West Haven, where I was born, is the Cranbury of my early books. It was a small town then, ideal for children, having open fields, woods, brooks, and hills and also lovely little beaches along the shore of the New Haven harbor, excellent for swimming, clamming, or taking off in a rowboat or canoe. Now West Haven is a big, sprawling suburb of New Haven, and the brooks and fields are gone. The Green, however, is still as it was, and the church, which figures in the Moffat books and in *Ginger Pye*, is as lovely as ever.

Due to my mother's and father's fondness for and interest in books, books have always been of prime importance in my life. My mother could quote profusely from many of the great poets; she was a fine storyteller, very dramatic in her presentations. I remember we older children had constantly to reassure my younger brother that the giant would not catch Jack and eat him up. Unconvinced, he always ran out of the room when that story was told. Mother had an inexhaustible supply of songs, stories, and anecdotes with which she entertained us while she was cooking dinner. We especially loved her stories of New York City, where she had been born and for which she was homesick always. Because of her stories of "little old New York," the city seemed like a second home to me when I went there to live.

I never really decided to write for children. It just happened that I did. I always wanted to become a writer, and I suppose it was because of my long association with children in various public libraries that I unconsciously directed my stories to them.

I don't know where I get my ideas. They come from childhood remembrances mainly. I revise my books again and again, trying to improve them all the way through the final proofs. I feel quite lost when a book is finished, and immediately start a new one.

Ginger Pye is about our old dog, one my brother and I had as children. He did get lost on Thanksgiving Day as a puppy and came back in May—grown up. Mr. Pye is based partly on my husband, Rice, and partly on my childhood remembrance of a certain man, the father of a friend, who was an ornithologist, very well known nationally but a modest, humble man whose importance the town did not suspect.

Mrs. Pye is based on many people too: partly my mother, partly my sister, partly myself—that is the timid, overanxious, have-you-got-your-sweater part—and partly made up. Rachel and Jerry are two children based on all the children I've known, as are all the child characters in my books.

In my writing I like to feel that I am holding up a mirror, and I hope that what is reflected in it is a true image of childhood that echoes the clear, profound, and unpremeditated thoughts and imageries of childhood. I like to make children laugh or cry, to move them in some way. I am happy that my books have been translated into many other languages, and I am grateful to the children everywhere who have looked into my mirror and liked what they have seen.

Irene Hunt

Irene Hunt, born on May 18, 1907, in Pontiac, Michigan, began teaching in the Illinois public schools in 1930, a career that became a lifelong interest. Her first book, Across Five Aprils *(1964), is a Newbery Honor Book; her second novel,* Up a Road Slowly *(1966; both Follett), received the Newbery Medal. She lives in Florida.*

My early childhood years were happy until my father died when I was seven years old. After his death, I was a very lonely child, living with grandparents until I was twelve. I lived on the farm mentioned in *Across Five Aprils*.

During the early 1960s, while teaching social studies to junior-high-school students, I felt that teaching history through literature was a happier, more effective process. Fascinated by the troubles of the border states at the time of the American Civil War, I saw a chance to help children see the many-faceted problems of that day. I hoped also to make children realize the need for critical thinking about social and political problems. My grandfather's poignant old stories had floated through my mind for years. Suddenly, I realized how they might be put to use. *Across Five Aprils* was generated by the needs of my students.

Up a Road Slowly was suggested by a memory that had haunted me throughout my adult life. I was one of a thoughtless group of children who once rejected a retarded child. Writing about Aggie was therapeutic for me—equal to a session in a psychiatrist's office. Other aspects of *Up a Road Slowly* were either autobiographical or experiences that had happened to others. I had long felt the need to tell girls that no matter what our age, the problems of growing up are universal.

I had very little formal writing training. One year while at the University of Illinois, I took a course in short-story writing. The letter Uncle Haskell wrote to Julie in *Up a Road Slowly* concerning her writing contains almost exactly the same comments made by my professor about my writing.

I believe I am one of those people who remember what it is like to be a child—the bewilderments and uncertainties as well as the joys. To write for children involves a close affinity with one's own childhood. If you have this, it follows that you will have that same affinity for childhood in general. You must remember!

Elizabeth George Speare

Elizabeth George Speare, born on November 21, 1908, in Melrose, Massachusetts, lived most of her life in New England. Her first book, Calico Captive, *was published in 1957, followed by* The Witch of Blackbird Pond *(1958), which received the Newbery*

Medal; The Bronze Bow *(1961), also a recipient of the Newbery Medal; and* The Sign of the Beaver *(1983; all Houghton), a Newbery Honor Book. In 1989 she received the Laura Ingalls Wilder Award. She died on November 15, 1994, in Tucson, Arizona.*

Since I can't remember a time when I didn't intend to write, it is hard to explain why I took so long getting around to it in earnest. After I graduated from Boston University, I became a high-school teacher, offering Shakespeare and Browning to a volcanic classroom. I don't suppose any of the students have ever remembered a word of what I tried to teach them, but I have never forgotten what they taught me. Surprisingly, in that first toughening year I discovered that I really *liked* teaching.

Calico Captive came about when one day I stumbled on a true story written in 1807 by Susanna Johnson, with a character who seemed to be an ideal heroine. For a long time this girl haunted my imagination, and finally I began to write down her adventures.

In order to truly share the adventures of my imaginary people, I had to know many things about them—the houses they lived in, the clothes they wore, the food they ate, how they made a living, what they did for fun, what things they talked about, cared about. You can call this research if you like, but that seems to me a dull word for such a fascinating pursuit.

Gathering the material for a book takes me a year or more. While I am taking pages of notes in libraries and museums, the story is slowly growing in my mind. When I finally begin to write, I know in general what my characters are to do and how their story will end, though many surprising changes always occur on the way. I work very slowly, doing only a few pages a day, trying to make each sentence say exactly what I mean. Sometimes I reach a blind spot, a sort of gulf, and for weeks I cannot see how I can possibly get my characters across to the other side where I want them to be. But sooner or later almost by magic a bridge appears. Some bit of history, some ancient custom, or perhaps just the sort of person one character has turned out to be suggests a way, and presently we are all safely across.

The Witch of Blackbird Pond was laid in Wethersfield, Connecticut, a very old town in which we had lived for twenty years. I was intrigued by an account from early New England history of English children who were sent from Barbados to Boston for an education. I wondered what would happen if a girl from that sunny and luxurious island had come not to Boston but to the small Puritan town of Wethersfield in 1685, with its narrow, hard life dominated by the meetinghouse. That imaginary girl became Kit Taylor in *The Witch of Blackbird Pond*.

For *The Bronze Bow* I went far afield from New England. I was teaching a Sunday-school class of seventh graders, and for all of us the life and people of ancient Palestine about which we were studying seemed very dim and far away. Actually the first century A.D. was an exciting, colorful, and violent age. To make the time come alive, I began to imagine a group of young people who grew up learning to hate their Roman conquerors, who longed for freedom for their country, and who heard and came to know the great Teacher of Galilee.

Young people often ask me why I always write about "olden days." To be honest, in my school days I was never very fond of history. But I have discovered now that when I follow the adventures of an imaginary family through some great events of the past, the pages of the history books come alive for me. I always find in my study of earlier days a new understanding of the present, and I come back to the things I know best with fresh perspective. I think that one of the great gifts that the past has to give to all of us, young and old, is this reinforcement of the spirit.

May Garelick

May Garelick, born in 1910 in Vobruisk, a small town in Russia, came to the United States with her family when she was nine months old. Working in publishing her entire life, she held various positions ranging from clerical worker to editor. She began writing children's books in 1951 and wrote many picture books. One of her most popular, Where Does the Butterfly Go When It Rains, *illustrated by Leonard Weisgard (Scott), appeared in 1961. She died on December 6, 1989, in New York's Greenwich Village.* Just My Size *(Harper, 1990) was published post-humously.*

I was just a baby when we came to the United States. We lived in New York City, and the elementary school I went to was probably the first school built there; it was called Public School 1.

After high school I went to college for two years. My family couldn't afford to keep me in school, so I quit and went to work, trying to continue my college education at night. It was too hard to work and try to be a good student. I had to work, so I gave up school. Of all the things I have done in my life, I feel this is the biggest mistake I ever made.

Maybe it is because I was brought up in a city that I became so aware of things in the country. As a child I wondered about a good many things, but I didn't ask questions; therefore, I grew up without knowing many of the answers. But I did develop a sense of observation and found out that you can always look up the answers if you know the questions. I wrote *Where Does the Butterfly Go When It Rains* to encourage children to notice things and ask about them.

It's funny: Children don't seem troubled by the question "Where does the butterfly go when it rains?" I've had a lot of trouble with grown-ups, though, who ask continuously, "But where *does* the butterfly go? Where? Tell me!" Children have given many answers voluntarily—"under a leaf," "under a rock," "in a tree." Really and truly, does it matter where a butterfly goes when it rains? No! But to think creatively, to make your own discovery, that's important. I write all my young nature books in response to a question. When I write, I always try to keep my audience in mind. I ask myself, What is it that the child wants to know about this? What is the *question*?

I have always child-tested my books. I go into classrooms to read my manuscripts to boys and girls long before they go to the publisher. I accept children's criticisms and enjoy their comments.

Ruth Krauss

Ruth Krauss, born on July 25, 1911, in Baltimore, Maryland, studied art and music at the Peabody Conservatory, graduated from the Parsons School of Fine and Applied Arts in New York City, and studied anthropology at Columbia University. The Happy Day, *illustrated by Marc Simont (1949), and* A Very Special House, *illustrated by Maurice Sendak (1953), are Caldecott Honor Books. She was married to Crockett Johnson (1906–1975), creator of the comic strip "Barnaby," author-artist of* Harold and the Purple Crayon *(1958), and illustrator of her book* The Carrot Seed *(1945; all Harper). She died on July 10, 1993, at her home in Westport, Connecticut.*

My whole childhood was spent drawing and making things. There was no television. I read all the time. I was writing since I was a kid. When I was fifteen, I wrote a book in a secret language that I hid from my parents.

My parents let me do what I wanted to do. I quit school after eighth grade so I could study art and the violin.

My first book was accidental. It was *The Good Man and His Good Wife*, illustrated by Ad Reinhardt, the famous nonobjective American painter; in 1962, Harper reissued it with drawings by Marc Simont. I was at Columbia University working on an anthropological project for Ruth Benedict on southern Italian farming families. Through a series of mess-ups and mix-ups she never received my work. I took a story I had written from the material to Harper's, the publisher. There were just two people in the children's department then, Ursula Nordstrom and Charlotte Zolotow. Ursula read the book, laughed, and said, "I'll take it!" I've written ever since. There is nothing like a taste of worldly success to start you on a career!

The Carrot Seed was my next book. I wrote it in forty-five minutes. It was the shortest book anyone had seen at the time. It has under one hundred words—about ninety-two. Actually, *The Carrot Seed* began as a 10,000-word story, which I simplified!

To do *A Hole Is To Dig: A First Book of First Definitions* [Harper, 1952], I went to the beach every day and would ask five- and six-year-olds the question, "What is this for?" or "What is that for?"—questions about things that children held personally dear to them. The kids thought I was crazy. I asked one boy what a hole is for, and he frowned and walked away from me. Another child, however, said, "A hole? A hole is to dig!" And that's how the title was born. I also collected material from kids at the Rowayton Public School and the Bank Street School.

Maurice Sendak had just brought in his sketchbook to Ursula at Harper. She showed me his sketchbook and I said, "That's it." He came to my house in Rowayton, Connecticut, and we did the book together. After that we did quite a few more together.

If I try to make myself sit down and write, nothing I like comes of it. I have no regular pattern for working. I can't call writing work for me; it's a form of play. I love it.

Virginia Sorensen

Virginia Sorensen was born on February 17, 1912, in Provo, Utah. A graduate of Brigham Young University, she began her writing career in 1942, with the publication of an adult novel, A Little Lower Than the Angels *(Knopf). In 1953 her first book for children,* Curious Missie, *appeared.* Miracles on Maple Hill *(1956; both Harcourt) received the Newbery Medal. She died on December 24, 1991, in Hendersonville, North Carolina.*

I was born in Provo, Utah, the third in a family of six children. When I was five, my family moved to Manti, a little town settled by Scandinavian Mormons. I'm sure my brother was right when he said we all felt obliged to be especially good and bright because our parents weren't active church people. But my mother wisely saw that we were baptized at the proper ages, so that we would really belong to the community. In Utah I was close to the history of my family's past. Several of my early novels were influenced by stories of the Mormon settlers that were passed down from my great-grandfathers, who came to Utah in the mid-1840s.

My own two children were grown up before I became interested in extension-library work and wrote my first book for children. After that I seemed to find children's stories wherever I lived. One was set in Utah, two in Pennsylvania, one in Denmark, and one in Alexandria, Virginia.

Miracles on Maple Hill was sparked by my moving to Pennsylvania. I was charmed by the seasons, especially spring and the first manifestation of it there—the rising of the sap in the trees in February. That delight and the Pennsylvania Dutch friends on a maple farm started the book going. The idea of rejuvenation happened later and made the eventual thread on which everything hangs.

After winning the Newbery Award, one is more prosperous and independent, but the demands grow—the speaking and so on. I found writing the next book very difficult; it took me *years*. Mostly it was a matter of not being able to satisfy myself. But this feeling comes to most writers as they grow older, I'm sure. Many writers tell me writing becomes harder and harder as they grow older.

I like to tell children that a story is a bouquet of things—places, people, ideas, plot—and no matter which you start with, all the rest must come in and make it a whole indivisible work.

Clyde Robert Bulla

Clyde Robert Bulla was born on January 19, 1914, on a family farm between Union Star and King City, Missouri. After several years as a writer of magazine articles and stories, he published an adult novel and then went to work as a columnist for a hometown newspaper. His first book, The Donkey's Cart, *appeared in 1946 (Crowell). Since then he has created many books for children, including novels, picture books, and nonfiction works. His autobiography,* Grain of Wheat: A Writer Begins, *appeared in 1985 (Godine). He currently lives in Los Angeles, California.*

My father married when he was twenty-nine, settled on a small acreage in northwest Missouri, and for the next forty-odd years went through the motions of farming. His heart was never in it. Mother was a homemaker, made do with little, and hoped for better things in life. Three children were born to them—two girls and a boy, what they had thought was a complete family. Nine years later I came along. I went to school in a one-room country schoolhouse. There was music in our home. There were books, although not many children's books. I read what was at hand—Dickens, Thackeray, an encyclopedia. I liked to wander about the farm, which was good-sized, and I got to know every tree and stone in the woods.

I never had any formal training as a writer. I began very young and proceeded by trial and error.

I like to carry an idea in the back of my mind for a while, allowing it to develop in its own way in its own time. One day, when the story seems complete, I begin writing; I write first in longhand, slowly and painfully. The opening paragraph is the hardest; sometimes I write as many as fifty or sixty before turning out one I can use. Every manuscript goes through several complete drafts. At times I have tried out my ideas on children. I hope the boys and girls know from my books that I have sympathy for them and that I remember what it is like to be a child.

Frank Bonham

Frank Bonham was born on February 25, 1914, in Los Angeles, California. After writing many adult western novels, he published his first children's book, Burma Rifles: A Story of Merrill's Marauders *(Crowell), in 1960. After that time he continued to write both adult and young-adult novels. He died in 1989 in California.*

I was born in Los Angeles, and raised there before smog and freeways. My father was born there also and his mother before him, in 1853. We moved around a little, trying to find a place where an asthmatic child—me—could breathe. Asthma was one of the big realities of my childhood. It never quite killed me, but it ended my college career, and I moved to a mountain cabin where I started writing. Indirectly I owe a lot to ill health. It kept me from becoming a third-rate newspaperman and forced me into a profession I love and for which I am suited.

My family life when I was a child was unremarkable, although both my grandfather and my mother were poets. I started writing for pleasure when I was about fourteen. I think I wrote out my dissatisfactions—just as a canary sings out of loneliness.

I studied composition in school and took journalism courses, but I don't think one can study writing as such. It's a matter of discovering one has a liking and a talent for working with words and developing it by hard work. A woman once asked Robert Frost when he decided to become a poet. He replied, "When did you decide to become a beautiful woman?" It just happens, but you can help the process along a little. Magic either happens or doesn't happen.

I had been writing twenty years when I discovered children's books. I was astonished and delighted to learn that almost any subject was a good one for children's stories, and after backing into the field, I continued to write mysteries, television scripts, and westerns. Many of my scripts were for such television series as *Wells Fargo, Shotgun Slade,* and *Death Valley Days.* But I soon found out that the real satisfaction was in writing adventure books for young people.

Durango Street [Dutton, 1965] started out as a story about white kids in a gang. But I soon learned that gang activity is largely just another aspect of racial discrimination. So to tell a story, a true story about what it was like to be born poor and black, I changed the original concept. White kids, at first, did not show much interest in knowing these things. However, black children immediately took the book to their hearts. I did research for about a year and a half on the background before beginning to write. Then I realized with panic that I had no plot. As soon as I turned on the faucet, the outline of the story emerged. Ten months of hard work went into writing this book. It has given me great satisfaction to know that the kids who are living the lives I describe in the book, or something close to them, are reading it and saying, "That's true!"

Young people today are concerned about far more things than was my generation. They not only grow taller today, they are taller inside, their minds are keener and more skeptical. Yet they are not adults, and the same child who lists *Cyrano de Bergerac* as her favorite play, and thinks *The Odyssey* simply groovy, may still be reading Nancy Drew.

How do you write for such a creature as this?

The question perplexes me every time I start a new story. Is the protagonist's problem a young child's or an adolescent's? Is it universal enough to interest many readers or only a few? Is it already old hat? Is my protagonist recognizable as a modern youth? Or is he so terribly modern that no one will recognize him two years from now? It is important to have an adequate range of literary staples for the young who are still in their prime reading years. Yet the minority child is offered too little that he will recognize as relevant to his world, his special problems, himself.

The fact that many of these youngsters are poor readers does not mean that one should engage in baby talk in writing for them. I make little conscious effort to simplify my vocabulary. Nor do I skimp my work, for "disadvantaged" does not mean "dumb."

The gratitude I feel for having spent fifty years doing work I enjoy is like a prayer.

William Armstrong

William Armstrong was born on a farm in the Shenandoah Valley near Lexington, Virginia, on September 14, 1914. Before writing Sounder, *his first novel for young readers and winner of the Newbery Medal (1969), he created a number of books on education and an adult novel,* Through Troubled Waters *(1957; both Harper). Since 1945 he has been a teacher at the Kent School in Kent, Connecticut. In 1972* Sounder *was made into a film starring Paul Winfield and Cicely Tyson.*

When I was four I learned the rudiments of reading in my mother's kitchen on a farm near Lexington, Virginia, from a man named Charles Jones, a black man who taught in the one-room Negro school in the area and worked on my father's farm. It was Charles Jones who told me the story of Sounder, the great hound dog—and he is the boy in my book.

Charles Jones was a man who had lived in such a furnace of affliction and opposition that every impurity had been smelted out of his soul. Nothing was left but purity. Tall, straight, with gray hair, there was a love shining from his eyes always felt by anyone he met.

Jones was a proud man, proud and dignified. My father had to work out elaborate excuses to do a simple favor for him, driving him to town after work or picking him up at school. They often broke bread together. That was something in Virginia seventy years ago. My father loved him. I did too. He died when I was in college, and it was as if a member of my immediate family had gone.

It was many years later, through the cold winter dawns on my farm in Kent, that I wrote the story of Sounder. So through the years, a memory lives, and one man's love and courage can become a legacy for another age.

I didn't know what the Newbery Award was, so there was no reaction on receiving it. I reread the book two days afterward to see if I could figure out *why* it had won. I didn't even know *Sounder* was a children's book until it was published. As a matter of fact, I don't even believe there is such a thing as a children's book.

Charlotte Zolotow

Charlotte Zolotow, born on June 26, 1915, in Norfolk, Virginia, attended the University of Wisconsin from 1933 to 1936. In 1936 she joined the children's books department at Harper. In 1981 Charlotte Zolotow Books became a new imprint at Harper. She wrote her first book for children, The Park Book, *in 1944. Since then she has created a wide body of work, including two Caldecott Honor Books:* The Storm Book, *illustrated by Margaret Bloy Graham (1952), and* Mr. Rabbit and the Lovely Present, *illustrated by Maurice Sendak (1962; all Harper). She is the recipient of both the 1986 Kerlan Award and the 1990 University of Southern Mississippi Medallion. She lives in Hastings-on-Hudson, New York.*

I was born on my sister's sixth birthday. She was pleased with the arrangement until she finally saw me. Then she cried and said she wished she had gotten a bicycle instead!

There were many books that were most important to me when I was young. One was *The Secret Garden* by Frances Hodgson Burnett. Anyone who reads my own work closely will find the influence it had on me. Another was *Heidi* by Johanna Spyri. In *Heidi* the loneliness and yearning of the child was so strong. I used to read it over and over again.

I began at Harper as an assistant to someone's assistant in the adult department, earning about twelve dollars a week! When Ursula Nordstrom took over the children's department, she asked me to join her. There were only three of us—Ursula, myself, and a secretary. Ursula made a lot of breakthroughs in children's books at every level—from picture books to books for young adults.

While working at Harper, I got an idea for a book I thought Margaret Wise Brown could write, about twenty-four hours spent in a park. I gave Ursula a long memo about it and she asked me to expand on it a little more. I went into more detail and she told me I had just written my first children's book! This lovely experience turned out to be *The Park Book*. It came out in 1944 with illustrations by H. A. Rey.

Mr. Rabbit and the Lovely Present started out as two books, but there was no emotional focal point in them, nothing that really made them work for a child, so I set them aside. Years later I heard my daughter ask somebody what she could get me for a present. The woman suggested that she go out and pick me a bunch of flowers. My daughter said, "Yes, I can get red ones and blue ones and green ones." Suddenly the idea for the book came together.

I'm terribly tuned in to children—their imagery, their minds, their freshness fascinate me. Their senses are so amazing because they don't have a judgmental sense of what is good and what is bad. They can like the odor of manure and hate the odor of a rose. The young child's mind is very much like a poet's mind.

A good picture book must be honest and unpretentious and direct. Whether it is humorous or poetic—or both, as some are—there should be some universal truth or feeling in it, and what Margaret Wise Brown called the "unexpected inevitable." I love the field of children's books because the author or artist dips into the freshness and originality of children, and these qualities are open to an infinite variety of theme and treatment.

Jean Fritz

Jean Fritz, born on November 16, 1915, in Hankow, China, came to the United States at the age of thirteen. Homesick: My Own Story *(Putnam, 1982), a Newbery Honor Book, chronicles her growing-up years in China. She is the recipient of the 1985*

Regina Medal, the 1986 Laura Ingalls Wilder Award, and the 1988 University of Southern Mississippi Medallion. In Surprising Myself *(Owen, 1993), an autobiography, she describes her daily life and how she writes. She lives in Dobbs Ferry, New York.*

As a young child in China I lived in the French concession, attended a British school, played with two German girls, and spent my entire childhood fighting a private revolutionary war in defense of my country. My chief opponent was a tough little Scottish boy with square knees and nasty things to say about George Washington. Communism and war moved to Hankow during our last years there. A shell fell in our yard on one occasion, a riot broke out in our living room on another, and my mother and I were repeatedly forced to evacuate. In 1928 we moved back to the United States.

I remember once when I was five years old standing at the door of my father's bathroom and watching him shave. In the bathroom was a big round bathtub, glazed green, that had a ladder for climbing in. As I watched my father, I announced, "I know what I'm going to be when I grow up. I'm going to be a poet."

My father's razor didn't flicker. "Well," he said, "that's fine. But you'll never make a living with poetry." I then decided I could write stories, too, stories about Americans. I left the bathroom and immediately wrote my first story about twins, American twins with an American bathtub, white and shaped for lying down.

The Cabin Faced West [Coward, 1958] was my first historical book. With it I discovered the joys of research. It was like exploring. Digging into American history also seemed to satisfy a need that I had, having grown up in China, of finding my roots, of trying to come to terms with just what it meant historically to be an American. After I had written it, I realized the story, although presumably about my great-great-grandmother, a lonely little girl in pioneer Pennsylvania, was really about me as a lonely girl in an equally foreign environment.

I am not one of those people who can mine for ideas. I simply stumble across them or do without. Once I have an idea, however, I worry it, lie awake with it, walk the floor with it, and make countless false starts before I can successfully launch it. I work an eight-hour day—not from discipline but because I can't put the story down. I work slowly, writing in pencil and typing it up at the end of each day's work; however, it is often not more than one or two typed pages. Rewrite? Of course I do.

Beverly Cleary

Beverly Cleary was born on April 12, 1916, in McMinnville, Oregon, and spent the first six years of her life living on a farm in Yamhill, Oregon. In Yakima, Washington, she became a children's librarian, which led her to write books for children. Her first book, Henry Huggins, *appeared in 1950. Among her numerous honors are the 1975 Laura Ingalls Wilder Award, the 1980 Regina Medal, and the 1982 University of Southern Mississippi Medal-*

lion. Ramona and Her Father *(1977) and* Ramona Quimby, Age 8 *(1981) are Newbery Honor Books. She received the Newbery Medal for* Dear Mr. Henshaw *(1983).* A Girl from Yamhill: A Memoir *(1988; all Morrow) describes her life and career. The mother of two grown twins, Malcolm and Marianne, she lives in Carmel, California.*

I loved living on a farm. Being an only child, I had to amuse myself. I rarely played with other children until I was six years old, when we moved to Portland, Oregon. Reading meant so much to me as a child. I had read many books about wealthy English children who had nannies or rode in pony carts. *We* knew only plowhorses! Other books I read were about poor children whose problems were solved by a long-lost rich relative turning up in the last chapter. I wanted to read funny stories about the sort of children I knew.

I was fortunate to have a teacher-librarian who suggested that I write for children when I grew up. This seemed like such a good idea that I decided writing for children was what I wanted to do. Making this decision while still a child was most fortunate, because I began to read critically while I was still reading from a child's point of view.

Unless you count an essay I wrote when I was ten years old (I won two dollars, because no one else entered the contest), *Henry Huggins* was my first attempt at writing for children.

Life with twins was busy! My novel *Mitch and Amy* [Morrow, 1967] came out of their experiences and the experiences of their friends when they were in the fourth grade.

Some parts of my stories come out right the first time; others I rewrite several times. I wouldn't dream of trying out my ideas on children or anyone else. A book should be the work of an author's imagination—not the work of a committee. If I start a book and do not like it, I just don't finish it. I don't try to be funny. Because of some lucky quirk in my personality, my stories turn out to be humorous. In my books, I write for the child within myself. Writing is a pleasure, and I feel that if I did not enjoy writing, no one would enjoy reading my books. If my books are popular with children, it is because my childhood was bounded by the experiences of an average American child, and I have been fortunate enough to make stories out of the ingredients such a childhood provides.

The awards I cherish most are those I have gotten from the votes of children; these are most meaningful to me because they come from my readers. Knowing that one's books really reach young readers is the most rewarding experience that can come to a writer of children's books.

Julia Cunningham

Julia Cunningham was born on October 14, 1916 in Spokane, Washington. After traveling most of her life, she settled in Santa Barbara, California, where she still lives. Her first book, The

Vision of François the Fox *(Houghton), appeared in 1960, a novel inspired by a visit to France. One of her popular novels,* Dorp Dead, *was published in 1965 (Pantheon).*

When I am working on a book, I make a valiant effort to sit down at my typewriter at the same time each morning, usually nine o'clock. I am able to concentrate effectively for only about an hour and a half and am lucky to come up with a page a day. The ideas come from anywhere—a conversation, a turn of someone's head, a fragrance, or simply a character walking into my imaginary life and taking over. I am not able to do much rewriting, at least not successfully, and am mostly an intuitive worker. The first draft must always be completely right.

I never had any formal training in writing. I just began at the age of nine and continued. I did have a wonderful English teacher in high school who did not interfere but encouraged me.

I have been asked for whom I write and the answer might be expected to be "for children." But that is untrue. I believe that basically most of us write for ourselves, not egotistically to hear ourselves talk but because of that other self, the one who enters any landscape of the imagination and is suddenly and totally involved with the lives of his or her characters. They appear from nowhere and hold center stage. They lead you, follow you, haunt you, occasionally club you to death, invite you to ride dragons, imprison you in an iron cage, and all of them, even the villains, befriend you. After all, who is telling the story? If the miracle has happened and you are at the core of this other reality, then they are telling the story.

A writer is a seeker who uses a typewriter instead of a schooner. He does it because he wants to. And each journey is an adventure, whether one returns with a bad cold and no money for a hot grog or, once in an inexplicable while, with a wreath of roses.

Matt Christopher

Matt Christopher, the eldest of nine children, was born on August 16, 1917, in Bath, Pennsylvania, and grew up in Portland Point, New York, near Ithaca. After holding a variety of jobs, he wrote his first book for young readers, The Lucky Baseball Bat, *in 1954 (Little, Brown). He has produced a wide body of novels for middle-grade readers centering around sports, one of his lifelong interests. Mr. Christopher lives in Rock Hill, South Carolina.*

My mother came from Hungary, my father from Italy. We spoke fractured English at home. My parents wanted to become Americans, and I sometimes felt ashamed that they weren't. It was a silly way to feel, since the parents of most of my friends were foreigners. As an adult I regret not having learned Italian or Hungarian.

My father worked at a cement plant, drawing wages barely sufficient to keep our large family in food and clothing. For a time we weren't able to afford a car. We had to ask neighbors to cart us to the doctor, about a ten-mile drive, whenever one of us became so ill that it worried our parents. We raised pigs and chickens, which helped supplement our meat supply, and in summers we had a garden, the pride and joy of my parents and grandfather, who lived with us. We played the usual games kids did at that time—Annie-over, lost turkey, duck-on-the-rock, and, of course, baseball, which we played with a tennis ball and broom handle.

At the age of fourteen I began writing poems and short stories. I wrote airplane and detective stories just for the fun of it during study periods in high school. At fifteen I began to play semiprofessional baseball, followed by some professional playing.

In 1937 I entered a national short-story-writing contest and won a prize. This proved to be the fatal bite of the bug! After writing scores of stories, I considered writing a book about baseball for young people. Frankly, I couldn't find one I really liked, or thought young people in the fourth or fifth grades would really like, so I tried doing one. *The Lucky Baseball Bat* was my first book.

I develop my books by first deciding what kind of story I plan to write—baseball, football, or some other sport. Then I decide on a nucleus, the main character's problem. The next step is to devise scenes applicable to the story, select names for my characters, write a plot outline, and then compose from it on my typewriter. After the first draft is written, I go over it about three or four times, polishing it, tightening it, making the story as suspenseful as I can, as plausible as I can. I am the main character in that story. I suffer and laugh with my main characters. I have witnessed incidents in baseball that I have used in my novels. The boy getting hit on the head by a pitched ball, for example, in *The Catcher with a Glass Arm* [Little, Brown, 1964], was based on an incident that happened to my nephew.

Writing still comes hard to me. I do a lot of revisions on each book. For me, the first draft is the hardest. After I've done that, I feel that ninety percent of my work is done. Revising is like putting frosting on the cake. It generally takes me two to three months to write a book, although I've done some in several weeks. In most of my books, action prevails. Recently, however, I've been doing more introspective writing. This helps to bring out the character.

For young people who want to write, I advise them to stick with it. Perseverance is everything. Don't be discouraged by rejections. I wrote forty stories before I sold one. If you like to write, if you've got writing in your blood, you will stay with it no matter what. It may not be easy. But it will be very gratifying.

Madeleine L'Engle

Madeleine L'Engle was born on November 29, 1918, in New York City. Since her first book, The Small Rain *(Vanguard, 1945), she has created a wide body of work, including the Time Fantasy series, beginning with* A Wrinkle in Time *(1962), a Newbery Medal winner.* A Ring of Endless Light *(1980; both Farrar) is a Newbery Honor Book. During a stint in the theater, she met and married the late actor Hugh Franklin. Much of her life is chronicled in several autobiographies directed to an adult audience.*

Recipient of the 1978 University of Southern Mississippi Medallion, the 1984 Regina Medal, and the 1990 Kerlan Award, she lives in New York City.

I am one of those rare creatures, a native of Manhattan. I was born shortly after World War I, an only child. My mother was a pianist; my father, a foreign correspondent and writer, was gassed during the war. I saw him dying for eighteen years; I led a rather isolated, lonely city life with lots of time to write, draw, and play the piano.

I attended a perfectly ghastly school that placed great emphasis on prowess in the gymnasium. My being lame didn't help me much in this institution. My homeroom teacher went along with the kids in labeling me the lame, unpopular girl in the school and also decided I wasn't bright. The last year I was there, they had a poetry contest in the spring that was to be judged by the head of the English department. The submissions went right to her without screening; otherwise, I wouldn't have had an entry. I won it, and there was great sound and fury because my homeroom teacher said, "Madeleine isn't bright. She couldn't have written that poem, she must have copied it." So my mother had to go to school with the mass of poems, novels, and stories I'd written, and they finally had to allow that I probably had written the winning poem.

When I became Mrs. Franklin, I gave up the theater in favor of the typewriter. Hugh retired too. We bought an old farmhouse in Goshen, Connecticut, and began to raise a family. We ran a general store there. We ran that store for many years, building it up from nothing to a flourishing business. Our customers included gypsies, carnival people, farmers, factory workers, artists, and philosophers. *Meet the Austins* [Vanguard, 1960] came directly out of our lives at that time; it could easily have been called *Meet the Franklins*.

A Wrinkle in Time was rejected by everybody—one publisher after another. I guess it was ahead of its time—too far out for children, they thought. Rather than becoming hysterical, as I sometimes did over my writing failures, I took this calmly.

Wrinkle was turned down for about the twentieth time just before Christmas. I was sitting on the bed wrapping presents and thought, "Madeleine, you've really grown up. You're being terribly brave about all this." I didn't realize until some time later, however, that I had sent a necktie to a three-year-old girl and some perfume to a bachelor friend!

Once it was published, *Wrinkle* did very well. It is still doing very well, and because of it my life certainly changed in all kinds of ways.

Is *Wrinkle* based on fact and did it really happen? Well, it happened in my mind, anyway, and if it isn't based on events in my own life, it *is* based on all the thinking I have ever done. Also, it is based on the scientific principles of Einstein's theories of relativity. By the way, as Mrs. Whatsit would say, there *is* such a thing as a tesseract.

I get my ideas from everywhere, everybody, and everything. I rework in that I rewrite and rewrite and rewrite, and each book gets more revisions than the previous one. I don't try ideas on anyone, but I do like to read bits and pieces of manuscript to people—either children or grown-ups, whoever is available. But not too much; an idea that is talked about too much seldom becomes developed in writing.

I think you must write constantly, whether you feel like it or not. I have kept copious, unpublishable journals since I was eight. Into the journals go everything I see, any ideas I have, pictures and anecdotes (which have been invaluable material for the Austin books). I think the journal is important, both to absorb self-indulgence and furnish source material. Experimentation with all forms of writing is important.

I am close to all my characters; they all have aspects of myself. They certainly have my flaws: shyness, stubbornness, problems at school, being misunderstood by teachers, being slow developers, having volatile tempers. Occasionally the flaws can be, perhaps, virtues. It was stubbornness that kept me going during the more than ten years when I was getting nothing but rejection slips. I *am* Meg Murray and Vicky Austin and Camilla and Philippa Hunter; and Charles Wallace? Well, he's the next son I never had!

Just because we reach adulthood does not mean that we need to leave the openness and enthusiasm and adventurousness of childhood behind us. In fact, to forget our childlike selves is to settle for being only part of a person.

Jean Craighead George

Jean Craighead George, born on July 2, 1919, in Washington, D.C., wrote her first book for children, Vulpes, the Red Fox, *in 1948.* My Side of the Mountain *(1959; both Dutton), a Newbery Honor Book, was made into a film. She received the Newbery Medal for* Julie of the Wolves *(Harper, 1972). Recipient of the 1982 Kerlan Award and the 1986 University of Southern Mississippi Medallion, she lives in Chappaqua, New York.*

I grew up in the wild edges and riversides of Washington, spending summers at the old family home at Craighead, Pennsylvania. My father, an entomologist who did work in Everglades National Park, taught me all the plants and animals, how to eat from the land, and to enjoy the wild freshness of the country. My twin brothers, Frank and John, who are most famous for their studies of grizzly bears in Yellowstone National Park, took me with them on hunting and camping trips, to the tops of cliffs to look for falcons, down the whitewater rivers to fish and swim, and over the forest floors in search of mice, birds, wildflowers, trees, fish, salamanders, and mammals. So absorbing and carefree were these excursions that my childhood in retrospect seems like one leaping, laughing adventure into the mysteries and joys of the earth.

I began writing in the third grade by a curious mishap. One day the teacher asked some of us children to go to the board to do arithmetic problems, and I couldn't do mine. So I wrote a poem on the board instead. When I sat down, I looked at all the arithmetic problems on the board and my poem. I thought, "Why did

I do that? My school career is over." But the teacher was understanding. She said, "Jean, that is a very good poem. Keep on writing." I did!

I took many English and writing courses during my school years. Fortunately I had several remarkable teachers who overlooked my bad spelling and punctuation for the feelings and ideas. At Pennsylvania State College I had the opportunity to study under the Pulitzer Prize–winning poet Theodore Roethke, who was my mentor. From him I learned to hunt down appropriate words of color and simplicity and to sense cavernous depths of nature in the small details of a blade of grass or a cricket wing with its timpani.

My ideas usually come in single words, like *seasons, migration*, or *living-off-the-land* (I consider that one word). Then I hassle the idea until personalities evolve to lead the story. Having gotten that far, I begin to write fast and furiously until I have a book, technically known as an outline. I put this away and, now familiar with the characters, events, and places, rewrite. I try this draft out on an editor or occasionally on children, but children are so nice they like anything you'll read or ask them about. Consequently I usually bounce ideas off adults who have good feelings about their own childhood. Then I rewrite and rewrite and rewrite. One of my books went through eight completely different drafts!

Many letters from children ask how I came to write *Julie of the Wolves*. While I was working as a freelance writer for *Reader's Digest* magazine, I asked them to send me to Alaska to do a story on the habitats of Arctic wolves. I flew, with my son Luke, to Barrow, Alaska, where scientists were studying wolves at the Naval Arctic Research Laboratory. As my plane came down the runway in this remote Eskimo town at the edge of the ice-filled Arctic Ocean, Luke and I saw a girl walking alone across the tundra. But I soon forgot her in the excitement of seeing wolves, snowy owls, seals, white foxes, walruses, and whales.

With the help of scientists, I talked to wolves in their own language just as they were doing, by mouthing noses, whimpering, howling, and standing tall.

Later I was invited to watch a wild pack of wolves with a scientist who was observing and studying wolves in Denali National Park. There, Luke and I lay on our stomachs on the alpine tundra to observe a large black wolf whom I named Amaroq—meaning *wolf* in Iñupiat, one of the Eskimo languages—and his wonderful pack. As we listened to him initiate the prehunt howl, saw him roll with the biffs from his energetic pups, and give directions with his eyes to his hunters, I knew I must write a story about a girl who is lost on the tundra and survives with the help of a wolf pack to whom she speaks in wolf language. That small figure on the tundra became Julie. Amaroq and his pack are themselves.

After returning to New York, I wrote an article for *Reader's Digest*. Guess what? It was *never* published.

I believe that if a child has a feel for writing and wants to write, there is an audience. Children should just dive in and go at it. I would encourage children to write about themselves and things that are happening to them. It is a lot easier and they know the subject better if they use something out of their everyday lives as an inspiration. Read stories, listen to stories, to develop an understanding of what stories are all about.

Mary Stolz

Mary Stolz, born on March 24, 1920, in Brooklyn, New York, grew up in New York City. Her first jobs included selling books at Macy's department store in New York and working as a secretary at Columbia University, which she attended for a while. Her stories first appeared in leading journals such as Ladies' Home Journal, Cosmopolitan, *and* McCall's. *Her first novel,* To Tell Your Love, *appeared in 1950.* Belling the Tiger, *illustrated by Beni Montresor (1961), and* The Noonday Friends *(1965; all Harper) are Newbery Honor Books. Recipient of the 1993 Kerlan Award, she lives in Florida.*

I discovered very early that words could be manipulated. It was possible to move them about, choose among them, find combinations of your own, and all exactly as you pleased. There is a sometimes almost unbearably exciting prospect offered by a sheet of blank paper and an idea.

In 1948, when I was living in New Rochelle, New York, I got sick with arthritis. I was in the hospital for three months and was very depressed. My doctor suggested that I write "something long." He was a good psychologist, and since he suggested that I write, I did. I wrote my first novel for young adults, *To Tell Your Love*. My doctor, Dr. Thomas C. Jaleski, also became my husband.

My editor at Harper was Ursula Nordstrom. Over the many years we worked together, we became close friends. She was a great editor, which was wonderful for her writers and artists. My own respect for her judgment led me to discard any manuscript that she really thought was unworthy. The way she put it was "Mary, this will lend no luster to your name or to Harper's." Naturally, I should like my work to be as lustrous as possible, so I listened to her and considered any unacceptable manuscript simply a finger exercise.

I love to write. It's an exciting, satisfying, frustrating, and altogether wonderful craft or art. I still get a thrill when I sit down and type "Page One, Chapter One." After finishing a book, I can still smell the foods I wrote about and I can see the family's furnishings in their various rooms. I know the characters as if they were friends. They're all still there—real.

In a picture book there can't be a syllable extra. It is the closest to poetry a prose writer can come. Children have much stronger sensibilities than adults. Children are still exploring and finding out about the world and about themselves. It keeps their sensibilities at high pitch. They detect dishonesty immediately.

Children ask me sometimes what book I'd take to a desert island, but I think I couldn't go to a desert island unless it has a public library on it!

Else Holmelund Minarik

Else Holmelund Minarik, born on September 13, 1920, in Denmark, came to the United States at the age of four. While teaching in a rural school in Commack, Long Island, she began writing books for children. Her first, Little Bear, *illustrated by Maurice Sendak, appeared in 1957. The team created three additional Little Bear titles, including* Little Bear's Visit *(1961; all Harper), a Caldecott Honor Book. She lives in New Hampshire.*

I began teaching during World War II, when there was a teacher shortage. I never felt that I had enough books to give my first graders that they could *really* read by themselves, quietly at home. I looked for such books and couldn't find them, so I wrote one. Actually, all I did was respond to the need of my little first graders.

I used bears as a vehicle for the simple reason that *I* could draw them on the chalkboard for the children. Bears have always haunted me throughout my whole life. When I was a child, a dream that kept recurring was one in which I was being pursued by a big bear. I would run and run but always woke up before the bear caught up with me. One night I got tired of running. I stopped. The bear stopped. And we began talking with each other. Ever since we've been good friends.

The same year *Little Bear* was published, Random House issued a similar type of series, Beginner Books. Their first title was *The Cat in the Hat* by Dr. Seuss. We both had the idea at the same time. It wasn't easy selling the idea at first, but look at how many easy-to-read books there are now!

Ursula Nordstrom, the children's book editor at Harper, asked Maurice Sendak to illustrate *Little Bear*. He made the book come alive so beautifully. I love the Victorian era. I live in an old

Victorian farmhouse, and Maurice just seemed to capture the Victorian way of life. He made Mother Bear Victorian with her costumes, her furnishings, her whole manner. The illustrations couldn't be greater.

Lloyd Alexander

Lloyd Alexander, born on January 30, 1924, in Philadelphia, Pennsylvania, wrote several adult novels before creating his first book for children. The Black Cauldron *(1965) is a Newbery Honor Book. He received the Newbery Medal for* The High King, *the fifth book in his Prydain Chronicles (1968; all Holt). Recipient of the 1986 Regina Medal, he lives in Drexel Hill, Pennsylvania.*

My family life when I was a child was unextraordinary. My childhood was certainly no more miserable than anyone else's, although at the time I thought it was. I learned to read quite young and have been an avid reader ever since, even though my parents and relatives were not great readers. I was more or less left to my own devices and interests, which, after all, may not be such a bad idea.

My first attempt at fantasy was *Time Cat: The Remarkable Journeys of Jason and Gareth* [Holt, 1963]. For over ten years I had been writing for adults and had never imagined I'd ever write for children. It wasn't until I was forty years old that somehow I began to sense that there were things I wanted to say that could best be said through books for young people. While doing historical research for *Time Cat*, I had stumbled across a collection of Welsh legends, the *Mabinogion*, which were medieval stories found in two manuscripts.

Here, it seemed, I recognized faces from all the hero tales of my childhood. My sense of Wales was of a land far more ancient than England, wilder and rougher hewn. The companions of Arthur might have galloped from the mountains and I would not have been surprised. Not until years afterward did I realize I had been given, without my knowing it, a glimpse of another enchanted kingdom.

I rework my manuscripts constantly and continually until I am more or less resigned to the fact that that's the best I can do at this particular moment. I don't try out my ideas on children. Story ideas seem to evolve from my own personal attitudes and ongoing explorations of life. I had no formal training in writing, but I did have the greatest teachers in the world—the great works of literature.

There is surely in the chronicles of Prydain as much of my own life as there is of ancient legends. My harp, still broken-stringed, is on my mantelpiece. Does it really belong to me or to the would-be bard Fflewddur Fflam, with his incorrigible habit of stretching the truth? Are the dreams of an awkward Assistant Pig-Keeper so different from mine as a child or those of all children? Or Gurgi's fearfulness, or Doli's striving for the impossible?

From what I've seen during my visits to schools, what children really want to know—and I think it's most important for them to know—is that writers are genuine human beings, that they're real people, with real lives, problems, ups and downs; that we're not abstractions or textbook figures. Even though we're adults, we really are alive.

On the level of deepest human feelings, I don't think there's all that much difference between grown-ups and children. The main difference, I believe, is that the child is still in the process of shaping his own view of life, of understanding himself and others, of working out his own attitudes and personality. One of the great things literature, and all art, can do is present different ways of looking at things, and help make some kind of sense out of the world.

Robert Burch

Robert Burch, born on June 26, 1925, in Inman, Georgia, attended public schools in Fayetteville, Georgia. After traveling around the world as a soldier during World War II, he began writing upon his return to civilian life at the age of thirty. His popular titles include Queenie Peavy *(1966) and the Ida Early series (all Viking), tales about an eccentric nanny/housekeeper. He lives in a rural area of Georgia in a house only two miles from the one in which he grew up.*

I was the seventh of eight children, six boys and two girls. Although a child of the Great Depression, I did not feel depressed. After all, everybody else was broke too. I learned early that material wealth really isn't important anyway, and we children had ourselves a pretty good time. We also had to work. Fayetteville in those days was a village, each family having its own livestock, and I made the mistake of learning to milk cows when I was in the fourth grade. The following year, when an older brother went away to college, I inherited his duties as the family's milkman, a job I held until I finished high school. Perhaps the work was good for me, but I'm awfully glad that today my milk comes from a case in the supermarket instead of directly from a cow.

I never base characters in my stories on real people. Some of them may be composites of people I have known, but I could never trace one of my characters back to a real person. Nor am I any of the characters myself, although often the setting and the economic circumstances of my stories are what I have known firsthand. *Queenie Peavy* is a character study of a type of person I've known, adult as well as child, who covers up deep-seated hurt with outrageous behavior. Such "chip-on-the-shoulder" individuals have always interested me. However, Queenie was not based on a real person. I might have used a boy as the central character, but a certain amount of the behavior would then have been dismissed by adults in the story as "boys will be boys."

Usually I begin a story by thinking of central characters. After I know them so well that they are real to me, I consider plot, wanting it to grow as naturally as possible out of character development and the circumstances of the time and place in which the story is set. Then I rush through the first writing, trying to get the story on paper as quickly as possible. You can be sure that my first drafts are drafty indeed; I can't always make sense of them myself! However, at that stage the real work has just begun. I spend months, sometimes years, rewriting, never entirely satisfied with a manuscript. I eventually reach a point at which I feel that I've done the best I can. It's time then to submit a story and take a few days off for a fishing trip before settling back to work again.

I'm pleased by any attention paid to my work and am delighted when one of my stories is singled out for special recognition, whether by adult selection committees or by children themselves. As a fond parent is happy when a son or daughter has made the honor roll, I'm naturally pleased when one of my books, in effect, has made good grades. But I'm equally proud of the ones who haven't, seeing them as the good-natured kids who will never make an A+ in their lives but who may be more fun to know and more comfortable to be around than their brighter siblings.

Zilpha Keatley Snyder

Zilpha Keatley Snyder was born on May 11, 1927, in Lemoore, California, and grew up in Ventura County, California. For nine years, she taught in public schools in different states, including California, New York, Washington, and Alaska. During her last year of teaching she wrote her first book, Season of Ponies *(1964). She is the author of three Newbery Honor Books:* The Egypt Game *(1967),* The Headless Cupid *(1971), and* The Witches of Worm *(1972; all Atheneum). She lives in Mill Valley, California.*

I was the middle child in a family of three girls. We lived in the country during the Depression and World War II. Due to shortages of such things as gasoline and money, I didn't get around much or do many exciting things. In fact, my world might have been quite narrow and uninteresting if it had not been for two magical ingredients—animals and books. We always had a lot of both. There was a library nearby, which to me was an inexhaustible storehouse of adventure and excitement.

I think I read almost a book a day during my childhood and loved every minute of it, so you can imagine that as soon as it occurred to me that books were written by ordinary human beings, I decided that was the kind of human being I'd like to be.

My teaching experience was invaluable to me as a writer. I not only met many wonderful students whose ideas, attitudes, or entire personalities have been inspirational to me, they also taught me to speak their language.

Washington School, where I taught, was a well-integrated school in a well-integrated neighborhood. There were good books available that were about minority-group children, but all I could find, for my grade level at least, dealt with racial problems—poverty, discrimination, and slavery. I began to look for a book that would encourage close and proud identification with a character who was of their own race and who would have exciting and wonderful adventures and face demanding problems. But the adventures and problems had to have as little as possible to do with race. I only wanted to give my minority children a happy and uncomplicated experience with a good book.

When I began to write *The Egypt Game*, I very soon knew for whom I was writing and for what purpose. Of course, I hope the story has things to say to children of all races and in classrooms of all kinds. If it does, it will be because the children in *The Egypt Game* are *real* children, and their relationships are real in schools like Washington—and could be in other places. Someday there will be more integrated schools where the problems of childhood can be the problems of childhood and have nothing to do with race.

My newest book is always my favorite one. It's like a new toy—because it isn't until later that you begin to see all the little faults and failures. However, I do have some special feelings about some of my books that don't change with time and the cooling off of creative fires. *The Velvet Room* [Atheneum, 1965] is one of those.

A long time ago I accepted the fact that I'm probably incurably superstitious, gullible, and generally unsophisticated. I've also known for some time that it's not too wise to admit that I still believe in fairy godmothers and some kinds of ghosts and all kinds of magical omens. I used to keep it a secret, but I don't think I will anymore.

Janice May Udry

Janice May Udry was born on June 14, 1928, in Jacksonville, Illinois. After graduating from Northwestern University, she worked for a year in a Chicago nursery school. She moved to Pomona, California, and then settled in North Carolina, where her husband taught at the University of North Carolina. Her first book, A Tree Is Nice *(1956), discovered in a pile of unsolicited manuscripts, brought Marc Simont the Caldecott Medal. The Moon Jumpers, illustrated by Maurice Sendak (1959; both Harper), is a Caldecott Honor Book. She lives in North Carolina.*

I grew up on a quiet, elm-shaded street in a small college town. I had no brothers or sisters, but there were plenty of relatives in Jacksonville. After graduating from college, I worked for a year in a nursery school in Chicago, Illinois. It was there that I became interested in the wonderful books for small children that were being published. I especially admired the books of Margaret Wise Brown. I decided to try to write a book of my own. *A Tree Is Nice* was it!

I am so fond of trees that I wanted everybody else to love them too. I remember the plum tree where I had my swing, where I played pirate ship, and where I had birthday parties when I was a child. I've seen children playing house in the shade of an inadequate bush when there was no tree in their yard.

At the time I wrote *A Tree Is Nice*, we were living in the heart of Valencia orange country in Southern California. Even more lovely than the orange trees, there are the big trees—the eucalyptus, the live oaks, the peppers, and the sycamores.

All of my books come from remembering my own childhood and from listening to and watching my daughters as they grew up. I sometimes read my manuscripts to them before sending them to publishers. *The Moon Jumpers* came directly from my childhood. I remembered the hot summer evenings in Illinois. No one had air-conditioning then, and being allowed to play outside after dark was delightful to me.

Let's Be Enemies [Harper, 1961], which also was illustrated by Maurice Sendak, is really a tongue-in-cheek look at children's quarrels. My older daughter, Leslie, used to say to me, "Tell me about a mean thing." I would then oblige her with stories about the meanest things I could think of. Leslie, of course, was delighted!

Betsy Byars

Betsy Byars was born on August 7, 1928, in Charlotte, North Carolina, where she grew up. Since she created Clementine *(Houghton, 1962), her first book for children, writing has been her main life interest. Among the many awards she has received are the Newbery Medal for* The Summer of the Swans *(Viking, 1970), and the 1987 Regina Medal.* The Moon and I *(Messner, 1992) is an autobiography written for middle-grade readers. She lives in Clemson, South Carolina.*

I was a happy, busy child. I started sewing when I was very young because my father worked for a cotton mill and we got free cloth. I was making my own clothes by the second grade, although I have a vague recollection of not being allowed to wear them out of the yard. I could make a gathered skirt in fifteen minutes. I sewed fast, without patterns, and with great hope and determination, and that is approximately the same way I write.

An English major, I graduated from Queens College in Charlotte, North Carolina, and right after graduation I married Ed, who was then a professor at Clemson University. I began my writing career by doing magazine articles to fill long hours while Ed attended graduate school at the University of Illinois. I had articles published in *The Saturday Evening Post*, *Look*, and *TV Guide*.

My goal was to write mystery stories. I never developed the ability to sustain a mystery, however, and would inevitably give the whole thing away on the second page. As my children grew, I became interested in books for children.

I always put something of myself into my books, something that happened to me. Once a wanderer came by the house and showed me how to brush my teeth with a cherry twig. That went into *The House of Wings* [1972]. *The Midnight Fox* [1968], my favorite book, was written when I, like Tom, saw a fox in the woods. The dog in *Trouble River* [1969] was my own dog, Sport. There is a lot of me in my characters, too. I particularly identify with Harold V. Coleman in *After the Goat Man* [1974; all

Viking]. When I was little, I had big feet for my age, and I gave those feet to Sarah in *The Summer of the Swans*.

The Summer of the Swans also grew from true-life experiences. I was asked to join a volunteer program to tutor some mentally retarded children. Although the character, Charlie, is not one of the children I tutored—he is purely a fictitious character—he was an outgrowth of the experience, and the book would never have been written if I had not come to know the children I was tutoring.

Winning the Newbery Award was a startling experience. At that point in my life I was not what you would think of as a professional-type writer. I knew very little about the publishing business; I had never been in an editor's office. I didn't even know any other writers. So this seemed the most astonishing thing that had ever happened.

Talking about my writing is difficult because I have no set rules for working. There is nothing I always do, nothing I try especially to avoid. Each book has a different experience. Sometimes I write a first draft straight through. Sometimes I write one chapter and work on it awhile before I continue. It takes me about a year to write a book, but I spend another year thinking about it, polishing it, and making improvements. I particularly enjoy writing books about boys and girls in the world today, because we are living in an exciting, lively period; young people are very bright, very individualistic. Over the years writing has become easier for me, more of a pleasure than work, so much so that I half expect someone to tap me on the shoulder and say, "Now if you could just take your writing *seriously*!"

E. L. Konigsburg

E. L. Konigsburg was born on February 10, 1930, in New York City and grew up in small towns in Pennsylvania. In 1952 she received a B.S. degree in chemistry from the Carnegie Institute of Technology in Pittsburgh, Pennsylvania. Her first book, Jennifer, Hecate, Macbeth, William McKinley and Me, Elizabeth, *published in 1967, became a Newbery Honor Book. Her second book,* From the Mixed-Up Files of Mrs. Basil E. Frankweiler, *published in the same year (both Atheneum), received the Newbery Medal. Until this time, no other author had been awarded the Newbery Medal and had a book designated a Newbery Honor Book in the same year. She lives in Ponte Vedra Beach, Florida.*

I wanted to write books that reflected the kind of growing up my own three children were experiencing while living in middle-class suburbia, because I have always regretted that when I was a child, there weren't any books that told what it was like to grow up in a small mill town, even though book jackets would promise that I would meet children in a typical small town.

Jennifer, Hecate, Macbeth, William McKinley and Me, Elizabeth was based on something that happened to my daughter, Laurie, shortly after we had moved. Laurie did not mix readily with other children. The girls in her class did not go out of their way to welcome a newcomer. It was only after a number of weeks had passed that Laurie came running into the house, asking to go to play at the home of a friend. With enormous relief I gave permission. I then looked out the window to see a tall, proud black girl striking off down the street, Laurie following with obvious respect. Two outsiders had found each other, and a friendship began.

From the Mixed-Up Files of Mrs. Basil E. Frankweiler came from three experiences; I read in *The New York Times* that the Metropolitan Museum of Art in New York City had bought a statue for $225. At the time of the purchase they did not know who had sculpted it, but they knew that they had an enormous bargain.

Shortly after that I read a book about some children who were captured by pirates. In the company of the pirates, the children became piratical themselves; they lost the thin veneer of civilization that they had acquired in their home.

The third thing that happened was a picnic that our family took while we were vacationing at Yellowstone National Park. There were no picnic tables or chairs, so my small group ate squatting slightly above the ground while groaning and complaining that the chocolate milk was getting warm, and there were ants and flies all over everything, and the sun was melting the icing on the cupcakes. This was hardly having to rough it, yet my small group could think of nothing but the discomfort. I thought to myself that if my children ever left home, they would never become barbarians even if they were captured by pirates. Civilization was not a veneer to them; it was a crust. Where, I wondered, would they consider running to if they ever left home? They certainly would never consider any place less wonderful than the Metropolitan Museum of Art with all those magnificent beds and all that elegance. And then, I thought, while they were there, perhaps they would discover the secret of a mysterious bargain statue and in doing so perhaps they would discover a much more important secret: the need to be different—on the inside, where it counts.

When I visit schools and talk to students about writing, I give them one word of advice and I give it to them quickly and loudly—FINISH! Starting something is easier than finishing it. You must have discipline to go from a few sentences, to a few paragraphs, to a piece of writing that has a beginning, a middle, and an *end*. Finishing something bridges the difference between someone who has talent and one who does not. My best advice? Apply the seat of your pants to the seat of your chair—and *finish*. FINISH!

I don't like to be asked if it is fun to write books. Writing books is just as it should be; sometimes it is fun, and sometimes it is simply frustrating. I think that is true of nursing or teaching or doctoring or house building or housewifery. But I know I would rather write.

Esther Hautzig

Esther Hautzig was born on October 18, 1930, in Vilna, then part of Poland. Her autobiography, The Endless Steppe: Growing Up in Siberia *(Crowell, 1968), describes the five harrowing years she and her family lived as prisoners in Siberia during World War II. She is a writer of diverse interests; her first book for children,* Let's Cook Without Cooking *(Crowell), appeared in 1955. She lives in New York City.*

After leaving Siberia at the end of World War II, I returned to Poland, a year of untold grief and misery for me. I was scared of crowds and noises—scared of my own shadow. I refused to venture out into the street for a long time. Perhaps I expected to be in some sort of heaven after the Siberian years. Instead I was thrust into a war-torn, largely bombed-out city where everyone still alive seemed, to my frightened eyes, to be in a desperate hurry to make up for lost time.

In 1947, at the age of sixteen, I left Poland for Sweden and finally sailed alone to the United States. On the boat to America I met Walter Hautzig, a concert pianist who was returning from his first tour of Europe. Luckily we both spoke German, so we were able to communicate. He later became my husband.

Upon arriving in New York City, I lived in Brooklyn with my aunt, uncle, and cousins. My cousins spoke to me *very* loudly and *very* slowly in the hope that in this manner I would learn to understand the English language!

I did not have a day of reckoning when I decided to write for children. I was working at T. Y. Crowell, the publisher, promoting children's books, when I wrote a cookbook in which the recipes did not need a stove; this turned out to be an especially good idea for a children's cookbook, so that is what it became.

After finishing another how-to book, *Let's Make Presents* [Crowell, 1961], I started working on *The Endless Steppe*, which had been in the making for some seven or eight years. I started the book in 1959; it was finally published nine years later. Whenever *Steppe* got too much for me, I'd make new curtains, or cover a headboard, or embroider some pillows or whatnot for our apartment—a wonderful antidote to writing.

Steppe was not easy to sell. It was submitted by my agent to adult-trade-book editors at first. They all wrote uniformly enthusiastic letters about the manuscript, but they were afraid that Americans would not be interested in reading about what happened in Siberia in the 1940s. An editor at a house in Boston, however, liked the book enormously and showed it to his children's book editor, who was anxious to publish it as a book for young adults. Since I was working at Crowell, I felt obligated to submit it there first.

I partly credit the late Adlai E. Stevenson for prompting the writing of the book. In 1959 he went to Russia and wrote a series of articles on his trip for *The New York Times*. One article was about Rubtsovsk.

I wrote a three-page, single-spaced, typed letter to him about my own experiences in Rubtsovsk. He answered, saying: "It was very good of you to write me, but I think you should write about life on the frontier of the Soviet Union during those trying war days. It would be a more useful contribution to our understanding than my pieces—and better literature."

I never had any formal training in writing, but sometimes I wish I did. Writing, and publishing, for children is an enormous satisfaction and challenge, for each time the writer writes, and the publisher publishes, one hopes that the new will become old, and then new again—and be enjoyed for generations. Because a writer is not creating for jaded cynics, but for human beings who savor life and listen to music, who look at pictures and read books with freshness and honesty, enthusiasm and perception, the writer of children's books is among the world's blessed creatures.

Mary Rodgers

Mary Rodgers was born on January 11, 1931, in New York City, and is known for the delightful scores she has written for musicals such as Once Upon a Mattress. *Her father, Richard Rodgers, was cocreator with Oscar Hammerstein II of such classic Broadway musicals as* South Pacific *and* Oklahoma! *Her first book for children,* The Rotten Book, *illustrated by Stephen Kellogg, appeared in 1969, followed by her first novel,* Freaky Friday *(1972; both Harper), which was made into a film by Walt Disney Studios. She lives in New York City.*

Although being born into a theatrical world sounds exciting and glamorous, it wasn't. My sister and I did not feel a part of it all. I had a regimented life, and the only way I could escape was to read and read and read. And I did! I read constantly. I used to pray for rainy days so my mother couldn't send me to the park. I read in the middle of the night. I'd wake up every single night at midnight and read until it was time to get up. My mother told her friends, "Mary is a child who tires easily." I would have to take a nap in the middle of the afternoon. It went on like this until I was twelve or thirteen years old.

I got into the writing of children's books in a curious way. I received a letter from Ursula Nordstrom, the children's book editor at Harper. At the time, I was having a discouraging time with the whole Broadway theater scene. I also had a husband and five kids who needed me. I decided that letter was a sign from somewhere. I went to see Ursula and Charlotte Zolotow, another editor at Harper. They told me to go home and put anything on paper that came into my head. I did. I sent about three typewritten pages of random notes in, and they turned out to be *The Rotten Book*.

My books are based on the "what if" principle. "What if you became invisible?" or "What if you did change into your mother for one day?" I then take it from there. Each book takes several months in the long process of writing, rewriting, writing, rewriting, and each has its own set of problems. The one thing I dislike about the writing process is the sometimes-loneliness of it all. Readers only get to see the glamor part of a bound book, not some of the agonizing moments one has while constructing it.

I had little to do with the making of the film *Freaky Friday*. The one thing I did want, suggest, and get was Jodie Foster to play Annabel.

The difference between a book and a film is that you can *savor* a book. When reading, you can stop now and then and think, but films keep rolling along. When those glamorous memories of a first night vanish, whether it's a Broadway opening or a film premiere, you can always turn back to the book. Books are within easy grasp. They're there!

Natalie Babbitt

Natalie Babbitt, born on July 28, 1932, in Dayton, Ohio, spent the first eighteen years of her life growing up in towns and communities throughout the state. The first book she illustrated, The Forty-Ninth Magician *(Pantheon, 1966), was written by her husband, Samuel F. Babbitt. She began writing in 1967 with* Dick Foote and the Shark, *a picture book in verse that she also illustrated.* Knee•Knock Rise *(1970) is a Newbery Honor Book.* Tuck Everlasting *(1975; all Farrar), a highly acclaimed modern fantasy, has been made into a feature film. She lives in Providence, Rhode Island.*

I was the younger of two children, and our family was a tight, secure, protective unit. My mother was an artist of landscapes and portraits, though she never felt she had the time and/or the right to become a real professional. She gave me invaluable help. I had a very happy childhood in spite of numerous moves and spent most of my time reading and drawing. I read mostly fairy tales and Greek myths, but my mother would read aloud every night from a list she somehow came by of the children's classics, which included everything from *Penrod* to *The Water Babies*. *Alice's Adventures in Wonderland* was read to me when I was nine; it has been my favorite book ever since.

I did not think originally of writing. I wanted only to be an illustrator. If I have had the courage to write, it is due entirely to the encouragement and support of my editor, Michael di Capua. Now I am far more interested in writing than in illustrating, though I still enjoy the picture-making process very much.

Knee•Knock Rise was a long time in the hopper. I wanted at first to do a simple picture book. It was to have been only a funny story, but it got away from me.

For some reason the story almost seemed to form and write itself. I felt no constraint in the vocabulary I used nor in saying what I wanted to say, though for that matter I seldom do. I am a firm believer in the perceptiveness and intelligence of children. The characters and the situation in Knee•Knock Rise were very real to me before I began to write. Perhaps this is because Knee•Knock Rise has a very simple, straightforward message. Nevertheless, I thought then, and still think, it is an odd sort of story; its success has been a great surprise to me.

With each new story, the pattern is much the same. It begins with a word or phrase that strikes some kind of sympathetic chord. I have an inordinate fondness for words and the alphabet. From this a group of characters evolves. The characters assume more and more positive personalities, and the events that follow stem from the actions and reactions they might logically be expected to have. I never seem to begin by saying to myself that I want to write about superstition, for instance. Goody Hall [Farrar, 1971] really began with my sudden affinity for the word *smuggler*. All the mulling takes place before a single word is committed to paper, and there is usually a great deal of research and rewriting. I like to present my editor with as polished a first draft as I can. I never try out my ideas on children.

Young people are the true and unfettered audience, and as such deserve the best effort of everyone who writes for them. Nothing can be good enough, but we can try.

Virginia Hamilton

Virginia Hamilton, born on March 12, 1936, in Yellow Springs, Ohio, wrote Zeely, *her first book for children, in 1966. Among her many honors are the Newbery Medal for* M. C. Higgins, the Great *(1974; both Macmillan) and three Newbery Honor Books:* The Planet of Junior Brown *(Macmillan, 1971);* Sweet Whispers, Brother Rush *(Philomel, 1982); and* In The Beginning: Creation Stories From Around the World *(Harcourt, 1988). Also the recipient of two Coretta Scott King Awards, in 1983 and 1986, the 1990 Regina Medal, the 1992 Hans Christian Andersen Award, and the 1995 Laura Ingalls Wilder Award, Ms. Hamilton lives in Yellow Springs, Ohio, with her husband, Arnold Adoff, a poet and anthologist.*

I grew up in Yellow Springs, the fifth child born to Etta Belle and Kenneth James Hamilton. Mother was the oldest daughter of a fugitive slave. Father was an outlander who once ran gambling halls in mining towns. He was charming, talented, moody, and forbidding. He was also the finest of storytellers besides being an exceptional mandolinist.

My mother's Perry family came to the town before Emancipation. The progenitor was, of course, a runaway slave. He settled down on the rich land. He married and prospered, and the family grew into the large, extended Perry clan. I grew up with the warmth of loving aunts and uncles, all reluctant farmers but great storytellers.

By the time I was seven, I knew that life must be freedom. Being the "baby" and bright, mind you, and odd and sensitive, I was left alone to discover whatever there was to find. No wonder, then, that I started to write things down at an early age. I'm a writer, I think, nearly by birth. There was no other way, really, that I could go.

Zeely came about via an old college chum working at Macmillan who remembered a short story I had written in college. She thought that if I tried making a book out of it, it would be a great story for children. Well, that's what I did! I took those eighteen moth-eaten pages and worked them over. It took a long time, but *Zeely* came from that.

I do not base any of my characters on real people. I do take the atmosphere of known people, their emotions, and give them to my characters. I think I'd have to say my characters are for the most part based on me. If you'll notice, every lead character is something of a loner, imaginative and contemplative, including Zeely, and Thomas Small in *The House of Dies Drear* [Macmillan, 1968], and Junior Brown. My characters are the way I see the artist, the *human*, isolated, out of time, in order to reveal himself more clearly. That is why Junior Brown futilely sees himself as the center of a wheel or spiral, trying desperately to find a place for his mental isolation.

The House of Dies Drear is so full of all the things I love: excitement, mystery, African American history, and the strong family. In it I tried to pay back all those wonderful relatives who gave me so much in the past. And I tried to show the importance of the black church to my being, also the land and the good and bad of small-town, rural life.

When I get an idea, I keep it to myself until I find out whether I have a good story working. When I know that, well, then, I'll read parts of it to my husband. A story idea simply comes to me, and I accept the wonder of that sort of thing without probing to find out where it comes from. Usually, though, I get a title in my head, like *Dies Drear* or *Junior Brown*, and then start thinking about it. I'm not aware of the thinking, for it is lightning swift. I get bits and pieces of conversation, flashes of atmosphere, a location. It's all a jumble at first, until I begin to write it and sort it out. I rewrite very little; when I'm ready to write it out, it comes along pretty clean.

I hope children and adults will accept my characters, all of them, in the manner they were given—with love and warmth for all that is uniquely human. A child—anyone—must know me through my books. I reveal myself only reluctantly, if at all. Not that I'm trying to hide, exactly, but more that I feel there is not really much to know. What I am is simply very personal and is revealed somewhat through what I write.

The past moves me and with me, although I remove myself from it. Its light often shines on this night traveler; when it does, I scribble it down. Whatever pleasure is in it I need to pass on. That's happiness. That is who I am. Even now, I fear nothing as much as a silent, moonless Ohio night.

Laurence Yep

Laurence Yep was born on June 14, 1948, in San Francisco, California. After attending Marquette University, he received a B.A. degree from the University of California in Santa Cruz in 1970, and a Ph.D. from the State University of New York at Buffalo. His first book, Sweetwater, *appeared in 1973. He is a third-generation Chinese American whose background is central to the themes of all his work.* Dragonwings *(1975) and* Dragon's Gate *(1993; all Harper) are Newbery Honor Books. He lives in San Francisco, with his wife, Joanne Ryder, an author of children's books.*

Growing up as a Chinese American in San Francisco, I found few books that dealt with my own experiences. I lived in an area where there were not many Chinese Americans and commuted by bus every day to a bilingual school in Chinatown. I felt like an outsider because I did not speak Chinese. Stories set on farms, in suburbs, or in midwestern small towns were less real to me than science fiction or fantasy. Science fiction and fantasy dealt with strategies of survival, people adapting to strange new lands and worlds, or some fantastic or alien creatures adjusting to ours. Adapting to different environments and cultures happened each time I got off and on the bus.

When I was eleven years old, I enjoyed Andre Norton's ability to conjure up other worlds; the world in her book *Star Born* was one of my favorites. For me, it was a spellbinding book in the fullest sense of the word. When I was fifteen, Ray Bradbury became another of my favorite authors, especially his *Martian Chronicles*.

At the age of eighteen, while a freshman in college, I sold my first story to the science-fiction magazine *Worlds of If*. I was paid a penny a word. The story took me about six months to write, and I earned a total of ninety dollars for it. It sounds like a lot of money until you consider how much time I put into that story. After it was published, I began writing science fiction for a living. I got four rejections for every acceptance. I took a lot of hard knocks from editors and publishers who told me I couldn't write, but I kept on.

I finally tried my hand at a children's science-fiction novel— *Sweetwater*. After it was published, it occurred to me that the aliens of the novel, the Argons, are similar in some ways to the Chinese in America. Out of *Sweetwater* grew *Dragonwings*, in which I finally confronted my own Chinese American identity.

For me writing is a long, hard, painful process, but it is addictive, a pleasure that I seek out actively. My advice to young writers is this: Read a lot. Read to find out what past writers have done. Then write about what you know. Write about your school, your class, about your teachers, your family. That's what I did. Each writer must find his or her own kind of voice. Finally, you have to keep on writing.

Fantasy and reality both play vital parts in our lives, for we may grasp with the mind and heart what we may not always grasp with the hand. It would be a tragic mistake to insist upon a realistic viewpoint to the exclusion of fantasy. Like the poet, we too must have rainbow wings of which we must be aware.

Robin McKinley

Jennifer Carolyn Robin Turrell McKinley was born on November 16, 1952, in her mother's hometown, Warren, Ohio. Because her father served in the United States Navy and merchant marine, she grew up all over the world. In 1975, she graduated summa cum laude from Bowdoin College. Afterward she held a variety of jobs—as a clerk in a bookstore, a freelance manuscript reader, and a barn manager on a horse farm. Her first book, Beauty: A Retelling of the Story of Beauty and the Beast *(Harper), appeared in 1978.* The Blue Sword *(1982) is a Newbery Honor Book;* The Hero and the Crown *(1984; both Greenwillow) received the Newbery Medal. She lives in London, England, with her husband, the writer Peter Dickinson.*

As an only child I grew up feeling that books, which you could take with you when your father was reassigned halfway across the world, were more reliable friends than human beings, who stayed behind or whose fathers got posted off in some other direction. I early found the world of books and reading.

I am clumsy, somewhat like Arien in *The Hero and the Crown*. Shortly before I was due to turn in *The Blue Sword*, a horse fell on me and broke my hand, thus bringing the book to a brutal halt for about six weeks.

About a month before I was to turn in *The Hero and the*

Crown, I fell on *myself* and broke my ankle. This was actually good for the book, because for nine weeks there was very little I could do but type. But I do now suffer from an interesting new paranoia and am planning to withdraw into a padded room with my typewriter as the due dates of new books approach.

Being with horses and listening to music are my favorite pastimes. I don't pretend to explain this; there are few things more real than mucking out stalls. As for music, the sun rises and sets in David Lee Roth, but my favorite real metal band is Motley Crüe. People fall back with cries of horror when I say this, but I believe my passion for heavy metal derives from the same source as my passion for opera; they are both about the excesses of human feeling, and they are both best loud.

I can't answer that inevitable question about where I get my ideas. Somehow or other some of these pictures in my head that more responsible people call daydreams turn themselves into stories. I am not an organized writer. When a story wants out of my skull and onto paper, it lets me know; it keeps me awake at night, makes me forget to pay overdue bills, renders me incapable of holding rational conversations with old friends.

Winning the Newbery Award paid the bills for two years! Writers tend to live from one advance or foreign rights sale or royalty check to the next. The Newbery is a great way to relax a little fiscally. It also means that you are taken more seriously as a writer, which is pleasant; it's not only the financial edge that writers find themselves teetering on. Personally, however, I did not find it much fun. I didn't like the bright lights and the attention; the Newbery clobbers the winner with an appalling burden of Having-To-Live-Up-To, which, I suspect, haunts you to a greater or lesser extent for the rest of your literary life. It's a two-edged sword, like just about everything in life.

I advise those who want to become writers to study veterinary medicine, which is easier. You don't want to be a writer unless you have no choice—and if you have no choice, good luck to you. You read as much as you can and write as much as you can. You don't have to be very organized about it unless you are an organized sort of person. But you *do* have to do it compulsively, convulsively, constantly—and you have to love it, to not be able to live without it. Neither the reading nor the writing is more important than the other. You read to feed your own story-telling faculty; you write to learn how, so that when the story you must get down on paper presents itself to you, you'll be ready. Well, you'll never be ready—the story in your head will always be better than what you write, which is one of the brutal facts about being a writer—but you can make yourself as ready as you can be.

Author-Illustrators

We write and rewrite, we draw and redraw . . .
—H. A. and Margret Rey

Sometimes a story idea comes to them first; at other times a sketch, drawing, or photograph sparks a marriage of word and illustration. These people face a double challenge—to bring both story and art to life for children.

James Daugherty

*James Daugherty, born on June 1, 1889, in Asheville, North Carolina, studied art at the Corcoran Art School in Washington, D.C., the Philadelphia Art Academy in Pennsylvania, and in London, England. During World War I, he worked in shipyards in New England, camouflaging ships for the United States Navy. After the war he painted murals for Loew's movie houses in various parts of New York City. He entered the field of children's books in the 1930s. In addition to two Caldecott Honor Books—*Andy and the Lion, *which he also wrote (1938), and* Gillespie and the Guards *by Benjamin Elkin (1956)—he received the Newbery Medal for* Daniel Boone *(1939; all Viking). He died on February 21, 1974.*

My earliest impressions are of the life and people on the farms in small towns of the Ohio Valley. My grandfather told stories of Daniel Boone and his buckskin men as he had heard them told—handed down by word of mouth and not from the books. My Virginia-born mother told tales of the Old South; my father read aloud from Shakespeare, Poe, and Dickens. As he read these wonderful adventures, I drew illustrations to go with the stories. My home, not school, gave me my best education.

My first book for children was commissioned by May Massee, who was the book editor at Doubleday Page Company; it was to illustrate Stewart Edward White's version of *Daniel Boone*. She told me, "Do what you like with it, have a good time, and God bless you."

Andy and the Lion began one wintry night as my wife, Sonia, and I sat by the fire in our Connecticut home, with the north wind howling in the treetops. We broke into laughter as we remembered the first New York performance we had seen many years ago of [Shaw's] *Androcles and the Lion*. All of a sudden Andy leaped into my mind's eye, and I drew pictures; the words came long after. *Andy and the Lion* has always been my favorite book because it was the most fun to do.

Nobody knows where ideas for books come from. I wish a consumer's guide or Yellow Pages could provide them. I am sure the good ones come from God if you ask Him. He does exist, you know. I don't try out my ideas on anyone. I am grateful that children read my books. To give them pleasure is a great privilege.

Elmer and Berta Hader

Berta Hader was born in 1891, in San Pedro, Coahuila, Mexico, and spent most of her youth in San Francisco, California. Elmer Hader was born on September 7, 1889, in Parjara, California, and was also raised in San Francisco. Throughout their adult lives they created books for children. Cock-A-Doodle-Doo *(1939) and* Mighty Hunter *(1943) are Caldecott Honor Books; the Haders received the Caldecott Medal for* The Big Snow *(1948; all Macmillan). Berta Hader died on February 6, 1976; Elmer Hader died on September 7, 1973.*

Elmer Hader

During my high-school years in San Francisco—poof—everything went up in smoke—literally! The big 1906 San Francisco earthquake and fire destroyed the whole city. After the fire had grown cold, what was once a lively city was now only a pile of broken brick and ashes. While San Francisco was rebuilding, I got a job firing a locomotive; I also served as a silversmith's apprentice and a surveyor's assistant.

I was fortunate enough to win a scholarship that took me to Paris, France. Badly in need of money to stay there, I worked for three years in a Paris vaudeville troupe. Soon after, the First World War came about, and I went into the army.

Berta Hader

Elmer and I met in San Francisco through a painter friend. I had a cottage for five dollars a month on Telegraph Hill. Elmer did a painting of Telegraph Hill, which now hangs over the fireplace of Laura Ingalls Wilder's house in Mansfield, Missouri.

Rose Wilder Lane, Laura's daughter, and I shared a four-story house in New York's Greenwich Village at one time. I was always friendly with the family.

In 1919, Elmer and I married on a shoestring. In order to make ends meet, we did illustrations for national women's magazines and newspapers that at that time had sections devoted to younger children. One of our friends was an editor on one of the magazines and liked an idea we had for a special children's page. This launched us into the field of illustrating for children.

During this period we did a series of drawings of Mother Goose rhymes. Our work in this area came to a halt when postal regulations caused the children's feature pages to be eliminated from the magazines.

This was a time when children's books were just beginning to come alive in the United States. I remember taking our Mother Goose drawings to Louise Seaman at Macmillan with the idea of putting them into a small book. Louise didn't know what to do with them. Harper took the book some time later but had to send to Europe to get prices—and some advice. Louise had great foresight, however, and it was she who encouraged and published our first books—a series called The Happy Hours. They were small, inexpensive picture books. We did about seven of them, and they established us in the field.

The Big Snow came about because of a disastrous snowstorm. When the real "big snow" came, we could barely see out of our studio window. Everything was completely covered.

I well remember the day when a member of the Macmillan staff called and said, "Berta, I've got the most wonderful news for you and Elmer." I replied, "Oh, I bet you're getting married!" The voice on the other end said, "No! Something better. You and Elmer just won the Caldecott Award!"

Marie Hall Ets

Marie Hall Ets was born on December 16, 1895, in North Greenfield, an area at that time a part of Milwaukee, Wisconsin. She created her first book, Mister Penny, *in 1935. Five of her books are Caldecott Honor Books:* In the Forest *(1944),* Mr. T. W. Anthony Woo: The Story of a Cat and a Dog *(1951);* Play With Me *(1955),* Mr. Penny's Race Horse *(1956), and* Just Me *(1965). She received the Caldecott Medal for* Nine Days to Christmas, *written in collaboration with Aurora Labastida (1959; all Viking). Recipient of the Kerlan Award in 1975, she died on January 17, 1984, in Florida.*

The happiest memories of my childhood are of summers in the North Woods of Wisconsin. I loved to run off by myself into the woods and watch for the deer with their fawns and for porcupines and badgers and turtles and frogs and huge pine snakes and sometimes a bear or a copperhead or skunk. When I was old enough to be trusted alone in a flat-bottomed boat, I used to explore the lake shore or the channels between the lakes.

Many of these childhood memories provided the storylines for several of my books.

After attending various schools, I went to San Francisco and married Milton Rodig, who died two months after our marriage. I went to Chicago to train for social work at the

University of Chicago. For my first job after training, I was assigned to a cost-of-living survey in the mountains of West Virginia, where I had to hunt out and visit isolated miners' shacks.

I later was sent to Czechoslovakia by the Red Cross and spent a year there in the mid-1920s organizing a permanent child-health program under the Czech government. I contracted a chronic illness while I was there, and when I returned to the United States, I had to make frequent trips to the Mayo Clinic in Rochester, Minnesota. To pass the long hours of travel, I wrote and drew pictures.

Nine Days to Christmas was written with my close friend Aurora Labastida. Aurora and I wanted to make a story about a little Mexican girl who lived in the city. Until that time it seemed as if American children's books portrayed all Mexicans as villagers wearing ponchos and following burros, when so many Mexicans, the majority, live in cities. In the book I used actual people as characters throughout, and the Mexicans' reaction was one of delight in recognizing themselves in the book as *real* people.

Gilberto, in *Gilberto and the Wind* [Viking, 1963], was a real child. I was vacationing in La Jolla, California, and actually looking for a model for a story. Walking down an alley was a young girl with a smaller boy. I knew this was the child I wanted to draw. The children disappeared. A few days later, while I was on the way to the bank, I walked down that same alley again, and I saw the boy! This time he was alone, and I was without my Kodak camera or drawing materials! Suddenly the child ran across the street and threw his arms around my knees. With my poor Spanish I managed to ask him to take me to his mother. He took my hand and led me to his house. The boy was

Gilberto. Actually, Gilberto chose me. His mother let me come to sketch him whenever I wanted to. I really came to know the family quite well.

The same family inspired *Bad Boy, Good Boy* (Crowell, 1967). By the time I wrote the book, the real Gilberto was about nine years old, spoke English, and went to a private school. I sent the family money from my royalties on the books to help keep him in school.

H. A. and Margret Rey

Hans Augusto Rey, born on September 16, 1898, in Hamburg, Germany, began drawing at the age of two. Margret Elizabeth Rey, also born in Hamburg, on May 16, 1906, studied at the Bauhaus in Dessau, at the Düsseldorf Academy of Art, and at an art school in Berlin. Years after they were married, the team created Raffy and the Nine Monkeys, *which was published by Gallimard in Paris, France, in the late 1930s. When the book appeared in the United States, the title was changed to* Cecily G. and the Nine Monkeys. *One of the nine monkeys in the story was Curious George, which led to the widely popular Curious George, series created by the couple and published by Houghton since 1940, the year the Reys came to the United States. H. A. Rey died on August 26, 1977, in Boston, Massachusetts. Margret Rey lives in Cambridge, Massachusetts.*

H. A. Rey

My family was rather stable and conservative, a pre–World War I middle-class family. Growing up, I lived close to the famous Hagenbeck Zoo and, as a child, spent much of my free time there. It is there I learned to imitate animal voices. I am proudest of my lion's roar, and once roared for three thousand children in the Atlanta Civic Auditorium, thus making the headlines in the *Atlanta Constitution* for the first—and last—time!

After World War I, I studied whatever aroused my curiosity—philosophy, medicine, languages—but never went to an art school. To pay grocery bills while studying, I designed circus posters, lithographed directly on stone, an experience that came in handy in later years when I had to do color separations for book illustrations.

In the late 1920s I accepted a job at an import firm offered to me by relatives in Brazil, selling bathtubs up and down the Amazon River! It took me twelve years to realize I wasn't on the right path in life!

Nineteen thirty-five was a turning point for me. It was when Margret, disliking Nazi Germany, fled to Rio, where I married her; we honeymooned in Paris, France, and spent the next four years there.

Cecily G. and the Nine Monkeys came about by accident. I had done a few humorous drawings of a giraffe for a Paris periodical. An editor at Gallimard, the French publishing house, saw them, called Margret and me, and asked whether we could make a children's book out of them. We did! Ever since then we have done mostly children's books, and it seems to agree with us. I have always been surprised at being paid for what I like to do best and would do anyway.

Basically I illustrate and Margret writes. She is a superb editor and critic of my artwork. Doing a book is hard work for both of us. People sometimes think we dash them off. We wish we could. We work very long on each one, frequently over a year. We write and rewrite, we draw and redraw, we fight over the plot, the beginning, the ending, the illustrations—as a matter of fact our work is nearly the only thing we do fight about.

Margret Rey

In June 1940, on a rainy morning before dawn, a few hours before the Nazis entered, we left Paris on bicycles, with nothing but warm coats and our manuscripts—*Curious George* among them—tied to the baggage racks, and started pedaling south. We finally made it to Lisbon, by train, having sold our bicycles to customs officials at the French-Spanish border. After a brief interlude in Rio de Janeiro, our migrations came to an end one clear, crisp October morning in 1940, when we saw the Statue of Liberty rise above the harbor of New York, and we landed in the U.S.A.

We took a small apartment in New York's Greenwich Village, rolled up our sleeves, and were ready to start from scratch. We did not know a single publisher, but before the week was over we had found a home for Curious George at Houghton Mifflin.

Among children we seem to be known as the parents of Curious George. "I thought you were monkeys too," said a little boy who had been eager to meet us, disappointment written all over his face.

We believe we know what children like. We know what *we* liked as children, and we don't do any book that we *wouldn't* have liked.

Edgar Parin and Ingri d'Aulaire

Edgar Parin d'Aulaire, born on September 30, 1898, in Munich, Germany, was an accomplished painter in Europe before coming to the United States and entering the world of books for children. Ingri Mortenson d'Aulaire, born on December 27, 1904, in Kongsberg, Norway, was also an artist of note. The couple met in an art school in Paris, France, in 1925. In 1929 they came to the United States. Their first book for children, The Magic Rug, *appeared in 1931. In 1932 they did the illustrations for the Newbery Honor Book* Children of the Soil: A Story of Scandinavia *by Nora Burglon. Their biography* Abraham Lincoln *(1939; all Doubleday) received the Caldecott Medal, and they were recipients of the 1970 Regina Medal. Ingri d'Aulaire died on October 24, 1980, in Wilton, Connecticut; Edgar Parin d'Aulaire died on May 1, 1986, in Georgetown, Connecticut.*

Edgar Parin d'Aulaire

Some people *say* I was born in Campo Blenio, Switzerland; my Swiss passport says so too! Switzerland was the legal residence of my parents, but actually I was born in a hospital in Munich, Germany. I grew up in almost all of the art centers of Europe—Munich, Paris, Rome, and Florence.

I started to draw and paint at a very early age, and I can't remember ever having had a stronger desire than to be left in peace to draw. My first picture book was made at the age of eleven or twelve; it depicted my American grandmother's adventures on the prairie being chased by Indians—my concept of what America was like.

At the age of twenty I got my first job from a publisher. I turned into a serious artist and only worked on illustrations for deluxe, illustrated editions, many with lithographs. I also painted frescoes on large and small walls in various countries.

The contrast of myself I found in a young girl, Ingri Mortenson, whom I met in an art school in Paris.

Ingri d'Aulaire

At the age of fifteen I revealed to my family that I had shown my paintings to the foremost painter in Norway, Harriet Backer; she advised me to start studying in an art school at once. My father, mother, and uncle backed me. After a great deal of art study in Oslo, Munich, and Paris, I came to the United States as Edgar and Ingri Incorporated!

The Magic Rug grew out of an illustrated letter to our niece in Norway. But it was the librarian Anne Carroll Moore, a true pioneer of the golden age of children's books, who opened our eyes to the field. With our vast training in the fine arts, both of us had the thought that working on children's books was a little below our dignity!

In doing lithography, you must be a bulldog and stick with it. Once we have started on a book, we know we must finish it. When one of us is down, the other is up. We may rewrite our text ten to twenty times before we are both satisfied, and hundreds of sketches end in the fireplace before the final drawings are executed. In all of our work we have used the old techniques of the artist-lithographer who did all his work by hand instead of using a camera, as most modern lithographers do. First, color drawings are sketched on paper in exactly the size needed. Next they are drawn on stone or zinc. The final color separations are combined on the finished stone; many additional tedious processes are still required to complete one lithograph. One's hand must be absolutely sure of every line, for there is no way to erase or to go over lines once they are drawn on stone or zinc.

Abraham Lincoln was born out of love. We wanted to try to make a wonderful man come alive for children, keeping all of his humility, gawkiness, and greatness. We followed the Lincoln path and pitched our tent wherever he had been staying, to smell the same flowers, be bitten by the same bugs, and have the same thunderstorms burst over our heads. Nearby farmers came out and invited us to come and stay with them if we could not afford to pay for a hotel in the nearest town. And we said, "Thank you, but we have to know what Abraham Lincoln first smelled and saw when he woke up at dawn." And maybe that is just what makes the book alive to children; you have to see it, smell it, hear it, really live it before you can tell the story of Lincoln. Children won't take half measures, and maybe that is why we love our work on children's books.

We have never had any problems working together as long as we remember that a plane needs a captain and a navigator. Then it is clear flying. Our goals as artists are so different, our individual paintings so different. But we have always respected each other *as* painters.

It is always difficult for two completely different artists to work together. We have created a third person, different from each of us, different from each other, but a combination of the two of us.

Dr. Seuss

Dr. Seuss, born Theodor Seuss Geisel on March 2, 1904, in Springfield, Massachusetts, received a B.A. degree from Dartmouth College in 1925. In 1937 his first book, And to Think That I Saw It on Mulberry Street *(Vanguard; reissued by Random House, 1989), appeared.* McElligot's Pool *(1947),* Bartholomew and the Oobleck *(1949), and* If I Ran the Zoo *(1950) are all Caldecott Honor Books. He is the recipient of numerous awards, including the 1980 Laura Ingalls Wilder Award, the 1982 Regina Medal, and*

a 1984 Pulitzer Prize. Dr. Seuss from Then to Now *(1986)*
appeared on the occasion of a retrospective exhibition covering
his sixty-year career, organized by the San Diego Museum of
Art. Daisy-Head Mayzie, *a posthumously discovered manu-*
script, appeared in 1995 (all Random). He died on September
24, 1991, in La Jolla, California.

My father worked as a city superintendent for the public
park system in Springfield, a job that included running
the local zoo. I liked the zoo animals, but in depicting them I've
used the Seuss system of unorthodox taxidermy. I've always
drawn, but I've never learned how. Back in high school, I did
have one art lesson, but I walked out of it. The teacher caught
me looking at a drawing upside down. I told her I was trying to
check the balance of the elements, but she didn't believe me. So
I never went back. I've capitalized on my mistakes. Since I can't
draw, I've taken the awkwardness and peculiarities of my nat-
ural style and developed them. *That's* why my characters look
that way.

In the fall of 1936, while aboard the S.S. *Kungsholm* on a long,
rainy crossing of the Atlantic, I amused myself by putting words
to the rhythm of the ship's engine. The words turned out to be
And to Think That I Saw It on Mulberry Street. Once ashore, I drew
pictures to go with it. The book was my first one; it was rejected
by twenty-six publishers before Vanguard Press accepted it. The
reason most given for rejection of the manuscript was that the
book was unlike other children's books on the market; hence,
its chance in the marketplace was slim!

Horton Hatches the Egg [Random, 1940] is the favorite of my books, probably for the selfish reason that it was the easiest to write. I had the most fun doing it. I was doodling around with drawings, the way I like to do, and a sketch of an elephant on some transparent paper happened to fall on top of a sketch of a tree. I stopped, dumbfounded. I said to myself, "That's a hell of a situation. An elephant in a tree! What's he doing there?" I brooded over it for three or four weeks, and finally I said to myself, "Of course! He's hatching an egg!" Then all I had to do was write a book about it.

I have no set pattern of working. Sometimes a doodled sketch contains a character I think is worth developing; sometimes a doodled couplet of verse suggests a dramatic situation. When I get a character who appeals to me, like Horton, I introduce him to another character and see what happens. When two characters get into conflict, the plot takes care of itself.

I never try out ideas on children. This, I feel, can be a terrible trap. Kids react too often to the *method* of presentation. You can charm them with a very bad story if you present it with proper salesmanship. Conversely, a good story fails if awkwardly presented. Some of the worst children's books ever published have been pretested with glowing results on captive audiences of kids.

The Cat in the Hat [Random, 1957], my biggest best-seller, was also the biggest pain to put together. I remember thinking that I might be able to dash the book off in two or three weeks. Was I mistaken! It ended up taking well over a year. To produce a sixty-page book, I may easily write a thousand pages before I'm satisfied. The most important thing about me, I feel, is that I work like hell—write, rewrite, reject, re-reject, and polish incessantly.

Writing books for kids is hard work, a lot harder than most people realize. And it never gets easier. I know my stuff all looks like it was rattled off in twenty-three seconds, but every word is a struggle—every sentence is like pangs of birth.

How do I feel about the enormous sales of *The Cat in the Hat*? Scared! Every time I start a new book, that cat squints at me and says, "Seuss, I bet you can't top me!"

A rhyme is something without which I would probably be in the dry-cleaning business!

Roger Duvoisin

Roger Duvoisin, born on August 28, 1904, in Geneva, Switzerland, came to the United States in 1925 with his wife, Louise Fatio. His first book for children, A Little Boy Was Drawing *(Scribner's), appeared in 1932. He received the Caldecott Medal for* White Snow, Bright Snow *(1947), and* Hide and Seek Fog *was named a Caldecott Honor Book (1965; both Lothrop). These two award-winning titles were both written by Alvin Tresselt. Among the many awards and honors Roger Duvoisin received were the Kerlan Award in 1976 and the University of Southern Mississippi Medallion in 1971. With his wife he collaborated on* The Happy Lion *(McGraw-Hill, 1954), the first book in a series of Happy Lion titles.* The Happy Lion *won the Kinderbuchpreis, the first award ever given by the West German government for children's books. He died on July 3, 1980, in Peapack-Gladstone, New Jersey.*

Throughout my boyhood I drew and painted. I began studying music at the age of seven, later attended the Geneva Conservatory of Music, and studied mural painting and stage-scenery design at the École des Arts Décoratifs. After finishing my studies, I worked at the Geneva Opéra Atelier des Décors designing scenery, painting murals, and doing posters and various illustrations. My love of ceramics led to managing an old pottery plant that Voltaire had founded in the little town of Ferney-Voltaire. I considered settling there, but the old manager of the pottery plant began to make trouble for me by breaking up all the pottery at night and mixing up the orders. One dark evening the old man even threatened to cut my throat. That's when I decided to leave—move to Lyon—where I took a position as a foreman of a large textile designing studio. I met the art director and president of Mallinson & Company, at that time one of the largest textile firms in America, and was offered a contract to go to New York to design textiles. Louise and I arrived in the United States during the Depression, and the textile firm went bankrupt soon after our arrival. I had no desire whatsoever to return to Europe.

Louise got the idea of *The Happy Lion* while traveling in France before the Second World War. A lion had escaped from a circus in a small French town. The peaceful wanderings of the well-fed lion through the streets of the town contrasted with the excitement he caused and was a natural subject for a book for children.

There are problems and great pleasures in collaborating. Louise has a sensitive eye. Her criticism is very valuable but sometimes difficult to accept, especially when she tells me that I should do particular illustrations all over again. She is usually right, though!

An award like the Caldecott Medal gives an artist some confidence and a greater sense of responsibility. I have always enjoyed illustrating Alvin Tresselt's books, because I share his love of nature, a love he expresses with charm and imagination in his poetic texts.

Munro Leaf

Munro Leaf, born on December 4, 1905, in Hamilton, Maryland, came to New York City in 1932 to work as a manuscript reader for several publishing companies. In 1936, at the age of thirty-one, he published The Story of Ferdinand, *illustrated by Robert Lawson (Viking). That same year,* Manners Can Be Fun *(Lippincott) appeared.* Wee Gillis, *illustrated by Robert Lawson (Viking, 1938), is a Caldecott Honor Book. He died on December 21, 1976, in Garrett Park, Maryland.*

I wrote *The Story of Ferdinand* in forty minutes on a rainy Sunday afternoon. I wrote it for Robert Lawson. I had known Rob for about two years. He was doing illustrations for children's books but was unhappy having to conform to publishers' ideas. I gave him *Ferdinand* and told him, "Rob, cut loose and have fun with this in your own way." I picked the story of a bull because dogs, cats, rabbits, and mice had been done thousands of times. The bull needed a name, of course, a Spanish name, so I took it right out of a fourth-grade textbook. Ferdinand was the name of the husband of Isabella, the queen who financed Chris Columbus's expedition in 1492. You can't get a more Spanish name than that!

Rob loved the manuscript. He took the book and completed the illustrations in two months' time. I brought the book to May Massee, the editor at Viking. She read it and said, "I'm locking this up in the safe!"

When the book came out, it got a great deal of publicity because the Spanish Civil War had started in June of that year. It was attacked by everybody! It was called "Red propaganda," a bitter satire of pacifism, on one hand, and a pro-Fascist tract on the other. I was greatly amused by the uproar, as was Rob. Neither of us had ever set foot in Spain, taken sides in the war, or even viewed a bullfight!

My wife, Margaret, ran the children's section in Brentano's bookstore in New York City. There was a young girl there who was employed to paint murals. Margaret thought she was quite good. "Write a story for her to illustrate," Margaret told me. I wrote a little story called *Noodle* about my neighbor's eleven-year-old dachshund. My neighbor was Hendrik Van Loon, who was the first author to win the Newbery Award, for *The Story of Mankind* [Boni and Liveright, 1921]. I gave the story to this young girl to illustrate, but the project didn't work out, and I put the story away. One day Ludwig Bemelmans, the author of the *Madeline* books, came into Brentano's to see how his book *Hansi* [Viking, 1934] was selling. My wife chatted with him. Soon after, he and his wife,

Madeline, came over to dinner. I told him, "Ludwig, I've got a story for you." I gave him *Noodle* and we became a team!

I also teamed up with another great guy, Dr. Seuss. We did an Army manual on malaria that was published in 1934 by the War Department entitled "This Is Ann." It was about the carrier of malaria, a nasty bug called anopheles mosquito!

Kids have been my patrons. I love kids. They've made my life worth living. If I weren't me, I'd envy me!

Hardie Gramatky

Hardie Gramatky was born on April 12, 1907, in Dallas, Texas, and spent his childhood years in Los Angeles, California. He began his art career with Walt Disney. After six years as an animator at the Disney Studios, he came to live in New York City, where he conceived Little Toot *(Putnam, 1939). He was an accomplished painter whose watercolors are in the permanent collections of such institutions as the Frye Museum in Seattle, Washington; The Chicago Art Institute; and the Kerlan Collection. He died on April 29, 1979, in Westport, Connecticut.*

After leaving high school, I got a job in a bank, worked as a logger and deck hand on a lumber schooner, wrote and illustrated a comic strip, and later turned to animating Mickey

Mouse! I always managed, however, to find time to develop my talent as an artist. Jobs helped me get through Stanford University in Palo Alto, and to the Chouinard Art School in Los Angeles.

When I moved to New York City, I had a studio in a loft overlooking the East River. It was a huge room with three big windows, and from these windows I would often see the little tugboats going up and down the river. *Little Toot* was conceived from this vantage point. I wrote and illustrated the story, but no publisher would accept it. It was rejected by every major house. One editor told me that it wouldn't be successful because children "aren't thinking this way this year"! I gave up on *Little Toot* and shelved it for a while. Finally, Putnam took it; it was their first book published for children. *Little Toot* is one of my favorite books, for it is the love story of a personality.

I have a great concern for boys and girls. They are the ones who can truly see the world the way it is. If I could reach just a few children through my work to make them greater people, I've done my life's work.

Don Freeman

Don Freeman, born on August 11, 1908, in San Diego, California, began his career sketching impressions of New York City's Broadway scene. His theatrical drawings appeared regularly in The New York Times *and the* New York Herald Tribune, *and he is the writer and illustrator of numerous books for children. Fly High, Fly Low (1957) is a Caldecott Honor Book. In 1975 the Margo Feiden Galleries in New York City hosted an exhibition of his work from the 1930s and 1940s. After his death on February 1, 1978, his wife, Lydia, found hundreds of sketches, drawings, and paintings that had never been published. Some of these appear in* The Day Is Waiting *(1980; both Viking) by Linda Z. Knab.*

I always wanted to draw and paint, so it is no wonder that shortly after finishing high school in St. Louis, Missouri, I set off for New York City. I got there by playing a trumpet in a jazz band, coming across the country doing one-night stands at dances, banquets, and anywhere else I could find a job.

When I got to New York, I studied at the Art Students League. I soon began drawing life in New York City, everything and anything I saw. Like my father, I loved the theater. I had little money, so I'd buy standing-room-only tickets to every and any show. I began drawing intimate glimpses of theater people and theater life—my personal impressions. I submitted several of my drawings to *The New York Times* and the *New York Herald Tribune*. They printed them!

I stopped playing the trumpet by accident rather than by choice. One night I was coming home on the subway and was so busy sketching that I didn't realize it was my stop until it was almost too late. I lurched out of the train, the doors closed behind me, and I realized I had left my trumpet inside. There I was pounding on the door! Losing my horn made me face the fact that I would have to make my living by drawing!

One evening when I was living in Greenwich Village, the playwright William Saroyan came to see me. He said, "I want you to illustrate my new book!" I thought I'd never hear from him again, but I was wrong. I did, and later I did the illustrations for his *My Name Is Aram* and *The Human Comedy*.

I got into the children's book field via a librarian-friend from California, Marge Raskin, who encouraged me to send in a book I did for my son. It was published, and I've been hooked ever since. I love the flow of turning the pages, the suspense of what's next. Ideas just come at me and after me. I work all the time. I don't know when time ends.

Several of my books reflect my love of New York City and the magic of theater. Two are *Pet of the Met* [Viking, 1953], which I did with Lydia, featuring one of my favorite characters, Maestro Petrini, the only mouse who works at the Metropolitan Opera House, and *Hattie the Backstage Bat* [Viking, 1970], who lives in the deserted Lyceum Theater.

I've always had a curious habit: When a book deadline draws near, I check into a hotel so that I don't become distracted. I've finished books in hotels in San Francisco, Los Angeles, New York City, and a host of other big cities. *Dandelion* [Viking, 1964] was finished in a gloomy hotel room in Washington, D.C.

Taro Yashima

Taro Yashima was born on September 21, 1908, in Kyushu, Japan. In 1939 he and his artist-wife, Mitsu, came to the United States. The first book he wrote and illustrated was The Village Tree *(1953).* Crow Boy *(1955),* Umbrella *(1958), and* Seashore Story *(1967; all Viking) are Caldecott Honor Books. The* New Sun, *an autobiography (Holt, 1943), describes his early years in Japan. Recipient of many awards, including the 1974 University of Southern Mississippi Medallion, he died on June 30, 1994, in Los Angeles, California.*

In Japan my father was a country doctor; my mother served as his assistant. After I graduated from the village school and high school, I went to the Imperial Art Academy in Tokyo for three years. I was always a rascal in school.

When I told my father that I was to be an artist, he was very pleased, for he believed that art is for humanity, just as his own profession was. Giving me money for a box of oil paints, he told me, "There are plenty of difficulties no matter what field you take. Step by step through difficulties, we learn how to develop."

My mother died when I was thirteen years old; my father, three years later.

After I married Mitsu and we had our first child, Mako, Mitsu and I came to the United States in 1939, so I could study art. When war was declared against Japan, we joined the war effort on behalf of the United States. I became involved with the United States Office of Strategic Services and I changed my name. My real name is Jun Atsushi Iwamatsu. I took the name Taro Yashima; it was the symbol of homesickness to me. *Taro* means fat boy, healthy boy; *yashima* means eight islands, old Japan, peaceful Japan.

Around 1951 or 1952, my daughter, Momo, began to ask me for a story. I began to seek my own stories—those inside me. A small tree stood in my earliest memories of childhood, almost as if it were a symbol of my childhood. I made *The Village Tree* for Momo. She appears in many of my books.

Crow Boy also stems from my recollections of childhood. In that story, as in all of my books, I get a hint of an idea through an inspiration from life. Sometimes this hint is as small as a poppy seed. I set up an envelope to collect any sort of material that seems connected with this seed. I think through the meaning of these materials until they ferment by themselves. The final fermentation is helped by researching, traveling, and reworking things over and over again.

Seashore Story was rooted in a trip back to Japan. Visiting there after twenty-four years, I felt myself as the character Urashima, the sad old man in the story. Every place I went to was so changed, all except my peninsula. This did not change, as it is, and always has been, so poor. Yet there was such a beautiful younger generation in Japan, much more than I had expected.

In *Crow Boy*, *Umbrella*, and *Seashore Story* my message was stronger than in any other of my books. I worked harder on them than ever before. And I guess, since they have been so well accepted, that people like them better than my others.

Leo Lionni

Leo Lionni was born on May 5, 1910, in Amsterdam, Holland, and spent his childhood years in Holland and Belgium. Before coming to the United States in 1939, he received a Ph.D. from the University of Genoa in Italy. He had a long career in the business world before writing and illustrating books for children. From 1949 to 1957, he was chair of the Graphic Design Department of the Parsons School of Design in New York, art director of Fortune *magazine, and president of the American Institute of Graphic Arts. His first book,* Little Blue and Little Yellow *(Obelensky), appeared in 1959. His four Caldecott Honor Books are* Inch by Inch *(Astor-Honor, 1960),* Swimmy *(1963),* Frederick *(1967), and* Alexander and the Wind-Up Mouse *(1969).* Frederick's Fables: The Leo Lionni Treasury of Favorite Stories, *published in 1985 (all Pantheon), contains thirteen of his popular picture books. He divides his time between New York City and a seventeenth-century farmhouse in Italy.*

As a child I lived within two blocks of two of the best museums in Europe. I spent most of my time there and quite naturally assumed that one day I would become an artist. In grade school, nature studies were very important to me. I remember how we collected plants and kept all sorts of animals; we drew leaves and animals. I relive these early experiences over and over again. I haven't changed very much.

Little Blue and Little Yellow, my first book, just happened by chance. I improvised a story I told to my grandchildren while riding on a train, made it into a dummy, showed it to Fabio Coen, a good publishing friend, who later became the children's book editor at Pantheon and Knopf. Fabio liked it—and published it! The book was successful. I was asked to do more and little by little discovered the joys of this profession, which was totally new to me.

I like to invent a technique for each of my stories. I have used drawings, crayon, collage, and gouache painting in various books. Since technique and style are naturally related, my style varies from book to book.

The important thing is the story. I eliminate many stories before I am convinced that I have the right one. Once the idea is clear, illustrating it is rather easy—the difficulties are always there, of course, but solving them is exciting. I deal with large themes; my books are fables and parables. They express something I think and feel.

Each book at the birth of its creative process has a moment. To shape and sharpen the logic of the story, to tighten the flow of events, ultimately to define the idea in its totality, is much like a game of chess. In the light of overall strategy each move is the result of doubts, proposals, rejections, which inevitably bring to mind the successes or failures of previous experiences.

If you can understand the rests, pauses, that are needed in a story, drama, music—also architecture and even conversation—then you can understand relationships. A successful artist is one whose work reflects the rhythms of life. You create tension, like silence, and you break it. I once asked a friend who is a flamenco guitarist just what it is that I like so especially about flamenco music, and he answered that perhaps it was that it asks a question and then answers it. These things come up in all the arts, and that is why I enjoy working in all of them.

Robert McCloskey

Robert McCloskey was born on September 15, 1914, in Hamilton, Ohio, and in 1932 attended the Vesper George Art School in Boston, Massachusetts. His first book for children, Lentil, *appeared in 1940. He is the recipient of two Caldecott Medals, for* Make Way for Ducklings *(1941) and* Time of Wonder *(1957).* Blueberries for Sal *(1948) and* One Morning in Maine *(1952) are Caldecott Honor Books, as is* Journey Cake, Ho! *which was written by Ruth Sawyer (1953; all Viking). In 1974 he received the Regina Medal. On December 4, 1987, at the 150th anniversary of the Boston Public Garden, a bronze sculpture of the mallard family from* Make Way for Ducklings *was dedicated with a plaque that reads: "This sculpture has been placed here as a tribute to Robert McCloskey whose story . . . has made the Boston Public Garden familiar to children throughout the world." On July 30, 1992, Barbara Bush and Raisa Gorbachev dedicated a replica of the Boston sculpture in Novodevichy Park near the Kremlin in Moscow. Robert McCloskey lives in Maine.*

I attended public school in Ohio, and from the time my fingers were long enough to play the scale, I took piano lessons. I started next to play the harmonica, the drums, and then the oboe. The musician's life was the life for me—that is, until I became interested in things electrical and mechanical. I collected old electric motors and bits of wire, old clocks and Mechano sets. I built trains and cranes with remote controls, my family's Christmas trees revolved, lights flashed and buzzers buzzed, fuses blew and sparks flew! The inventor's life was the life for me—that is, until I started making drawings for the high-school paper and the high-school annual.

As a young man I painted for two summers on Cape Cod, during which time I never sold an oil painting, only a few watercolors at most modest prices, and financially my art career was a bust. I took a bread-and-butter job doing a form of commercial art I had little interest in.

I went to call on May Massee, editor of children's books at Viking in New York City. I came into her office with my portfolio under my arm and sat on the edge of my chair. She looked at the examples of "great art" that I had brought along (they were woodcuts fraught with drama). I don't remember *just* what words she used to tell me to shelve the dragons, Pegasus, and limpid pool business, and learn how and who to "art" with. Some time later I went to see May Massee again, this time with my new-styled drawings and a story about a boy and his harmonica. She took the book. *Lentil* was born.

While making huge murals of famous socialites from Boston's Beacon Hill for the Lever Brothers Building, I noticed the ducks who were part of the Boston Public Garden scenery. It was then that the idea of *Make Way for Ducklings* evolved. As the idea began to take shape, I researched and studied the habits and the anatomy of mallard ducklings in every conceivable way. I sketched them in the Garden, observed stuffed specimens in the American Museum of Natural History in New York City, and even sought the aid of an ornithologist at Cornell University. When I felt I needed live models, I went to the old Washington Market in New York City and bought four squawking mallards; two of them turned out to be fakes!

The noise, especially in the early morning, led to many complaints from the neighbors. The ducks, which I kept in the bathtub, splashed all over the place; the lady downstairs complained of leaks in the ceiling. For a few weeks I crawled on hands and knees after them with my sketch pad—and a box of tissues! The ducks never stood still. I had to slow them down somehow so I could make the sketches. The only thing that worked was red wine. They loved it and went into slow motion right away!

The letters I get from children fall into several categories. One category is pictures of ducks sent to me from the world over—from California to Scandinavia, from Holland to Turkey. The same situation exists everywhere, I guess—ducks and duck traffic!

Then hardly a day goes by without my getting a question about *Homer Price* [Viking]. In the first story I referred to four robbers. While I was being inducted into the Army, the book was in production. I hadn't reread the story after the publisher asked me to do another drawing. I drew it, and drew five robbers! The whole thing was simply a matter of bad arithmetic! That book came out in 1943, and I still get kids writing to me telling of their "discovery."

Brinton Turkle

*Brinton Turkle was born on September 15, 1915, in Alliance, Ohio.
He attended the Carnegie Institute of Technology in Pittsburgh,
Pennsylvania, and studied art at the School of the Museum of
Fine Arts in Boston, Massachusetts, the Vesper George Art School,
and the Institute of Design in Chicago, Illinois. After working
in the theater and advertising, he wrote and illustrated his
first children's book,* Obadiah the Bold *(1965).* Thy Friend,
Obadiah *(1969, both Viking) is a Caldecott Honor Book. He
lives in Santa Fe, New Mexico.*

I was always drawing. Unfortunately, none of my school-
teachers appreciated it. If only one elementary-school
teacher had egged me on, I think I would have acquired art
skills much earlier than I did. In senior high school, I used to
sit in a history class and copy pictures of people such as Marie
Antoinette and Napoleon. The teacher of this class encouraged
me to draw, and I did. I learned more about history that year
than I ever did before.

I never wanted to do any kind of artwork other than illustrating
books. At the end of four years at the School of the Museum of
Fine Arts, I went to New York City and walked into May
Massee's office at Viking with a portfolio of drawings, including
illustrations for a story I had adapted from a folktale. Miss Massee

leafed through the portfolio, looked at my story with breath-taking speed, and said, "I think you will be doing children's books one day. When you have some new things I'd like to see them."

I was out on the street blinking in the June sunshine before I realized Viking wasn't ready for me. After several unsuccessful tries at other places and some time in Chicago, where I worked in advertising, I went off to New Mexico to think things over, start a family, and to make a dubious living illustrating texts and a few trade books.

The character Obadiah began as a valentine to a very small friend in Chicago. I drew a picture of a redheaded boy dressed in old-fashioned Quaker clothes, shyly holding a valentine on which was written, "Will thee be mine?" From the first he looked as if he should have a story. A long time after that, while I was on a brief holiday in Nantucket, lodged in an eighteenth-century inn, the Quaker influence on the island came to me as a complete surprise. After dining too well on lobster, I awoke in the middle of the night with a stomachache and a story— *Obadiah the Bold*.

Back in New York, I showed it to Ezra Jack Keats, who urged me to take it to Annis Duff at Viking. She took it!

Ezra Jack Keats

Ezra Jack Keats, a self-taught artist born on March 13, 1916, in Brooklyn, New York, designed murals and book jackets before illustrating books for children. He received the Caldecott Medal for The Snowy Day *(Viking, 1962);* Goggles *(Macmillan, 1969) is a Caldecott Honor Book. Recipient of many awards, including the 1980 University of Southern Mississippi Medallion, he died on May 6, 1983, in New York City, where he had lived his entire life.*

I was the youngest of three children who grew up in Brooklyn during the Depression years. I drew from the time I was four years old. I first realized that my drawings meant something when one day I covered our enamel-topped table with a host of sketches. My mother came in, and I expected her to say, "What have you been doing?" or "Get the sponge and wash off that table!" Instead she said, "Did you do that? Isn't it wonderful?" She then proceeded to look at each drawing, clucked her tongue, and said, "Now isn't that nice!" Then she said, "You know, it's so wonderful, it's a shame to wash it off." So she got out the tablecloth we used only on Friday nights, and she covered the whole little mural.

My father was a waiter in a Greenwich Village beanery. He did not give me the same open encouragement that my mother did. He was painfully aware of how difficult the life of an artist could be. He objected to the time I spent drawing and painting—because I might neglect my schoolwork, but above all because if I became an artist I would live a life of neglect, deprivation, and starvation.

One day he came home and tossed a big, fat, unused gleaming tube of oil paint on the kitchen table and said, "See how artists starve? One of those guys came in and swapped me this tube of paint for a bowl of soup." This began to happen with some frequency. It was clear to me then that he was buying all this stuff he brought home but just couldn't admit it.

Years later after I had grown up, my father suffered a fatal heart attack away from home, and I went to identify him. As part of the procedure, the police asked me to look through his wallet, and I found myself staring deep into his secret feelings. There in his wallet were worn and tattered newspaper clippings about the awards I had won. My silent admirer and supplier had been torn between dread of my leading a life of hardship and real pride in my work. He had never acknowledged my work or spoken to me about my painting, except to grumble about the foolishness I was pursuing.

About 1956, while exhibiting my paintings at the Associated American Artists Gallery in New York, I was asked to do a jacket for a novel by Vita Sackville-West. Elizabeth Riley, an editor at Crowell, the publishers, saw the book and asked me to do a jacket for a juvenile novel. She liked what I did and suggested that I illustrate a children's book. It was *Jubilant for Sure* by E. H. Lansing [Crowell, 1954]. I suddenly found my field—one which fused my feelings for children, storytelling, and painting.

The Snowy Day turned my life around. I had been illustrating books by other people showing the goodness of white children, and in my own book I wanted to show and share the beauty and goodness of the black child. I wanted the world to know that all children experience wonderful things in life. I wanted to convey the joy of being a little boy alive on a certain kind of day—of *being* for that moment. The air is cold, you touch the snow, aware of the things to which all children are so open.

The idea of using collage came to me at the same time I was thinking about the story. I used a bit of paper here and there and immediately saw new colors, patterns, and relationships forming. When I finished the book, I myself was startled.

When I got the call to tell me I had won the Caldecott Medal, I didn't know what it was. I began asking my friends in the field, "What's the Caldecott Award?" After several had told me about its importance, I floated way up there in space.

To me, one of the greatest triumphs in doing a book is to tell the story as simply as possible. My aim is to imply rather than to overstate. Whenever the reader participates with his own inter- pretation, I feel that the book is much more successful. I write with the premise that less is more. Writing is not difficult for me. I read into a tape recorder, constantly dropping a word here and there from my manuscript until I get a minimum amount of words to say exactly what I want to say. Each time I drop a word or two, it brings me a sense of victory!

After *The Snowy Day* was published, many, many people thought I was black. As a matter of fact, many were disappointed that I wasn't! The book brought me a host of joys, but also a few woes. Once when I was asked to speak and autograph books in a southern town, a man came up to me and asked belligerently for the *white* edition of *The Snowy Day*. Accustomed to such remarks, I merely smiled and said, "Like life, there is only one edition."

The greatest source of material for my books is that I am an ex-kid. We all have within us the whole record of our childhood. What I do is address the child within myself, try to be as honest as possible, and then hope for the best.

Ashley Bryan

Ashley Bryan, born on July 13, 1923, in New York City, attended both Cooper Union and Columbia University in New York. He is an artist of note, whose first illustrated book for children, Moon, for What Do You Wait?, *a book of poems from the work of Rabindranath Tagore selected by Richard Lewis (Atheneum), appeared in 1967. He has worked as a folklorist to preserve African American heritage; this is reflected in such volumes as* Walk Together Children: Black American Spirituals *(Atheneum, 1974),* I'm Going to Sing: Black American Spirituals, Volume II *(Macmillan, 1982), and* All Night, All Day: A Child's First Book of African-American Spirituals *(Atheneum, 1991). He won the Coretta Scott King Award for his book* Beat the Story-Drum, Pum-Pum *(Atheneum, 1980). His book of original poetry,* Sing to the Sun *(Harper, 1992), received the first annual Lee Bennett Hopkins Award, given by the Children's Literature Council of Pennsylvania. In 1994 he received the University of Southern Mississippi Medallion. He lives in Islesford, on a small island off the coast of Maine.*

I cannot remember a time when I have not been drawing and painting. In elementary school I began to make books. My first books, made in kindergarten, were illustrated ABC and counting books. At that time the entire book production was in my hands—from start to finish. I was author, illustrator, binder, and distributor. These one-of-a-kind "limited editions" drew rave reviews from family and friends and were given as gifts on all occasions.

I made books for members of my family to give as birthday presents, Christmas gifts, or any time—from Valentine's Day to Harriet Tubman's birthday! That feeling for the handmade book is at the heart of my bookmaking today, even though my originals are now printed in the thousands, and I no longer have to distribute them myself!

I got into illustrating books, and later writing them, by way of Jean Karl, editor at Atheneum, who came one day to my New York studio. I really didn't know why she was there and kept showing her pieces and pieces of my various artwork. I didn't know she was there to offer me an opportunity to illustrate a book for children. I will always be indebted to her and her insight.

African American spirituals are religious songs of an enslaved people. Varied Western influences merged with the slaves' profound African musical heritage to give us these songs.

Using biblical themes close to their own experiences, these people sang of the human need for dignity, recognition, joy, and freedom. These songs come to us today, through generations of singing African Americans, with undiminished force and significance.

My work in drawing and painting has kept me close to the

images evoked by the spirituals. I have often done drawings that seemed to come right out of one of the songs. It was natural, then, that I should plan one day to begin work illustrating the spirituals.

For many years my friend Dolores Koenig, a librarian from Milwaukee, Wisconsin, would write and ask me if I had started *the* book of songs. "We need that book," she said. I began work on *Walk Together Children* after receiving a proverb from her: "God admires me when I work, but He loves me when I sing."

I did many drawings on visits to Antigua in the West Indies, the island from which my parents had come to New York after World War I. Some of these drawings were the basis for my illustrations.

The interior of my cousin's bakeshop is the scene for "Let Us Break Bread Together." It looks the way bread shops did centuries ago, and as they still are in places where the dough is kneaded by hand and baked in wood-fired stone ovens. From drawings of donkeys and the occasional donkey carts that I saw, I drew the illustration for "Swing Low, Sweet Chariot." Sketches of the small shacks surrounded by patchwork fences were used for "My Good Lord's Done Been Here."

Whenever I am invited to share my tales, I *always* read first from the works of African American poets—Gwendolyn Brooks, Nikki Giovanni, Paul Laurence Dunbar, and Langston Hughes— *always* Langston Hughes. Their poems allow me to demonstrate the vocal play that I carry over into the stories. Two books that demonstrate this influence are *The Dancing Granny* [1977]— which is dedicated to the memory of my granny, Sarah Bryan, who danced *all* the time whenever she heard any kind of music and who would utter, "The music sweet me so"—and *Turtle*

Knows Your Name [1989; both Atheneum], a retelling of a story from the West Indies.

African tales are a beautiful means of linking the living Africa, past and present, to our own present. What the African sees in his world, the questions he asks, the things that he feels and imagines, have all found their way into our stories.

There is a poem by the Senegalese poet Leopold Sedar Senghor in which he unites childhood to Eden, present to past, life to death, with the line *"un pont de douceur les relie"*—"a tender bridge connects them."

That lovely phrase stays with me as I retell and illustrate African stories. I hope that my work with the African tales will be, by the very nature of storytelling, like a "tender bridge" reaching us across distances of time and space.

Peter Spier

Peter Spier was born on June 6, 1927, in Amsterdam, Holland, and came to the United States in 1952, after serving in the Royal Dutch Navy and working for a number of years as a reporter for Elsevier's Weekly, *Holland's largest magazine. His first book for children,* The Cow Who Fell in the Canal, *by Phyllis Krasilovsky, appeared in 1957.* The Fox Went Out on a Chilly Night *(1961) is a Caldecott Honor Book. He received the Caldecott Medal for* Noah's Ark *(1977; all Doubleday). Recipient of the 1984 University of Southern Mississippi Medallion, he lives in Port Washington, Long Island, New York.*

I grew up in Broek in Waterland, a small romantic village that Americans know as the setting for *Hans Brinker, or the Silver Skates* by Mary Mapes Dodge. I cannot remember a time when I did not dabble with clay, draw, or watch someone draw. My father, illustrator and journalist Jo Spier, worked at home, so I grew up with it all.

At the age of eighteen I decided art would be my career and went to the Rijksacademie, an art school, in Amsterdam.

I design my books from beginning to end. First I visit the locale where the book takes place. I call this my journalistic quest. To do *London Bridge Is Falling Down* [Doubleday, 1967], I went to England to gather material. I can't make things come alive from photographs, travel posters, or looking at *National Geographic* magazines. I must become a part of the location I am to draw!

To begin a book I first make accurate pencil sketches. Then I do ink sketches and finally watercolors. A book takes anywhere from four months or more to finish, working steadily sixteen hours a day. I put in long hours at the drawing board and a lot of hard work until a book is completed.

An illustrator is like a writer; they both have a certain arsenal at their disposal—memory, imagination, and feeling. An illustrator must extend this arsenal to draw trees as trees are seen in life— high trees and low trees. He must make the people in his books come to life, as well as the stores and stones; the unimportant

details become quite important if you are going to be exact—
and you *must* be *exact*.

Ellen Raskin

*Ellen Raskin, born on March 13, 1928, in Milwaukee, Wisconsin,
spent her childhood there and attended the University of Wiscon-
sin in Madison. In 1949 she moved to New York City to work as a
graphic designer and illustrator. Prior to writing her first book,*
Nothing Ever Happens on My Block *(Atheneum, 1966), she
illustrated over a thousand book jackets. She was the author and
illustrator of sixteen books for children.* Figgs & Phantoms
*(1974) is a Newbery Honor Book; she received the Newbery Medal
for* The Westing Game *(1978; both Dutton). She died on August
9, 1984, in New York City.*

My father, Sol Raskin, was a pharmacist; my mother,
Margaret, a housewife. I have one sister two years
younger than I. I was a child of the Depression. I was very
bright in school, had few friends, was an avid reader and a
dreamer (see *Nothing Ever Happens on My Block*). I had to wear
glasses and thought I was ugly (see *Spectacles* [Atheneum,
1968]). We lived in a four-room apartment frequently visited by
my mother's large family (see *Ghost in a Four-Room Apartment*
[Atheneum, 1969]). I played the piano from the age of four and

loved it (see *Songs of Innocence* [Doubleday, 1966]).

Nothing Ever Happens on My Block started with the doorbell ringing and a water-falling-on-the-head incident that actually happened to some children on our block when my daughter was young. Once I started to do the story, the rest just came.

My training in writing came from reading a great deal. I studied art at the University of Wisconsin and had worked ten years as a commercial illustrator. Writing comes much easier for me than illustrating, for writing is just ideas; after a character has been delineated, all that is necessary is the name. In illustration, after the idea comes consistency in drawing. The same characters have to appear page after page, and tons of research has to be done for every book.

 I am often asked where I get my weird ideas. I'm not really sure where they come from. I sit down at my typewriter with a wisp of an idea and a few names. As I write, the characters appear, the plot unfolds (not what I had in mind at all) and my book takes shape. Then I rewrite and rewrite. And rewrite!

Only after my book is done do I recognize the characters as people I have known. In fact, to my surprise, *Figgs and Phantoms* turned out to be my autobiography. The characters are masked by humor, and true incidents twisted by imagination, but I am, indeed, Mona Lisa Figg Newton. On the other hand, I am also the very different Angela Wexler in *The Westing Game*. Why these weird disguises? Perhaps I want my readers to have a good time with my books. Or maybe I'm just out-and-out mad.

Maurice Sendak

Maurice Sendak was born on June 10, 1928, in Brooklyn, New York. Illustrating books in the early 1950s, he established his reputation as a major force in children's literature with his drawings for A Hole Is to Dig *by Ruth Krauss (1952). He received the Caldecott Medal for his book* Where the Wild Things Are *(1963). He illustrated the Caldecott Honor Books:* A Very Special House *by Ruth Krauss (1953);* What Do You Say, Dear? *by Sesyle Joslin (1958);* The Moon Jumpers *by Janis May Udry (1959);* Little Bear's Visit *by Else Holmelund Minarik (1961);* Mr. Rabbit and the Lovely Present *by Charlotte Zolotow (1962); as well as the two Caldecott Honor Books that he also wrote—*In the Night Kitchen *(1970) and* Outside Over There *(1981; all Harper). He is the recipient of the 1970 Hans Christian Andersen Award, the 1981 University of Southern Mississippi Medallion, and the 1983 Laura Ingalls Wilder Award. In the early 1990s he established The Night Kitchen, a national theater for children. He divides his time between Ridgefield, Connecticut, and New York City.*

I had always wanted to be an artist. My sister, Natalie, gave me my first book. I can still remember the smell and feel of the book's binding. My brother, Jack, and I were always making books together. Jack would write, I would illustrate, and our mother would proudly show the finished products to all the neighbors. We did about twelve books together, and we loved it.

Where the Wild Things Are is an example of how I felt as a child. It is a child's level of seeing things. Adults find the book fearful; however, they misinterpret childhood. Children find the book silly, fun to read, and fun to look at. This, I feel, shows the gulf between childhood and adulthood.

Hector Protector and As I Went Over the Water [Harper, 1965] has in it my feeling for the dance and my love of music; it captures all of me. It was a keystone book in my life and is one of the most meaningful to me. It was a difficult book to do. I took a simple four-line verse that is of no great consequence; then I had to expand and enlarge it, make variations on a theme, and make it my own. Many people think I actually wrote the text. Hector is my kind of kid. He's Max in *Where the Wild Things Are* and he's Pierre, the hero of one of the four books in my Nutshell Library [Harper, 1962]. Children identify with him, particularly boys.

I have no fixed ideas when I work, beyond, "I'm going to work today." When I have a project, it's quite incoherent. Actually, the creative process is total chaos. The only order is what you create and the discipline you bring to it. Creativity is an individual kind of thing.

When I write, I write sporadically, and I write everything in my head. I write steadily until I am finished. Illustrating is quite different; it is more routine, a process that comes to me naturally.

When I did *Little Bear* [Harper, 1957], I wanted Mother Bear to be an image of warmth and strength—nothing less than motherhood itself. So I dressed her in a Victorian costume because those voluminous skirts, the voluminous sleeves, and her voluminous figure all made for the strong and comforting tenderness I wanted her to exude. And when Little Bear sits in her lap, I had her envelop him. The folds of her skirt surround him. There couldn't be a safer place in all the world than in Mother Bear's lap.

I write books that happen to be, for reasons unknown, more appropriate for children. I believe we have created an arbitrary division between adult and children's books that does not exist. Lewis Carroll didn't set out to write for children. He was writing *books*. What I write takes as much intense effort, as much creativity and dramatic sense, as the so-called grown-up books.

Aliki

Aliki Liacouras, born on September 3, 1929, in Wildwood Crest, New Jersey, has illustrated over a hundred books, including many titles in the Let's-Read-and-Find-Out Science series (Harper). She also writes fiction, nonfiction, and biography. She lives in London, England, with her husband, Franz Brandenberg, a children's book author.

I was born on Labor Day during my family's seaside vacation, but lived and grew up in and near Philadelphia, Pennsylvania. My parents were born in Greece, and we were raised in a tightly knit family and community that upheld Greek traditions. My father was a grocer and work was a way of life; my parents' goal was their children's education. Our interests won their praise, attention, and encouragement. I now know that these, headed by love, are the ingredients of Quality Parenting.

Ours was a musical family. I showed early talent and played the piano by ear, but my future was sealed when I was five, when my kindergarten teacher told my parents: "She's going to be an artist someday." I had drawn a portrait of two families, each with three girls and a boy—ours and Peter Rabbit's. We all studied music, but I breathed art. I drew constantly, even through math classes. After I graduated from the Philadelphia College of Art, I freelanced in various art fields—display, advertising (my main pursuit)—and for a time, I had my own greeting-card line.

On a trip to Florence, Italy, I bought a dictionary from Franz Brandenberg, and a year later I married him. For three years we lived in Switzerland, where Franz was born. During that time I wrote *The Story of William Tell* [Faber, 1960].

In 1960 we returned to New York City, where I pursued advertising. Through a series of coincidences I found myself illustrating books and realized that doing them perfectly suited my temperament. Eventually my writing took two distinct directions—fiction, which comes from within, and the "research" books that began in earnest in 1969 when Franklyn M. Branley, editor of the Let's-Read-and-Find-Out Science series, said, "Why don't you write a book about dinosaurs?" and I said, "Because I know nothing about them." He answered, "GREAT!"

In 1977 we moved to London, and I now divide my time

unequally between London, New York, and Switzerland. I work my head off, since work is my life—more my life than my career.

About my name? Children ask me, "Do you have a last name? Do you have a mother and father?" I tell them Aliki is Greek for Alice and that I use one name because a clever friend suggested I do so for professional purposes. Aliki is a good name, and my married name, Aliki Brandenberg, sounds like something you would see in a medical book!

Ann Grifalconi

Ann Grifalconi, born on September 22, 1929, in New York City, taught in junior and senior high schools there for ten years. After co-authoring Camping Through Europe *with Ruth Jacobsen (Crown, 1963), she began illustrating and writing books for children.* The Jazz Man *(Atheneum, 1966), written by her mother, Mary Hays Weik, is a Newbery Honor Book;* The Village of Round and Square Houses *(Little, Brown, 1986) is a Caldecott Honor Book. She lives in New York City.*

As a child I lived in Greenwich Village, over an artist's studio. A sculptor lived there who was working on a marble bust of Joe Louis, the famous prizefighter. My brother John and I used to see Mr. Louis come and go, day after day. We watched a huge block of marble take on a resemblance to the famous champion fighter. Maybe my love for art and for drawing minority people started there.

I find each culture filled with beautiful people with strong features and very expressive faces. My interest in poor children reflects a great deal of my own childhood experiences. I was a Depression baby, and I well remember the Depression days. It seems that we ate and almost lived on evaporated milk and chopped meat. Mother was a great cook, though, and made wonderful meals from this combination. There were times, though, that we didn't have even that. I remember well how Mother once fainted from hunger. I never knew what a steak was until I was an adult!

I worked my way through Cooper Union doing all kinds of odd jobs. I folded laundry in a Laundromat, worked with children in various organizations, and even demonstrated paint-by-numbers sets at a five-and-ten-cent store right in the heart of Times Square. I had to leave that job because I really didn't believe in this type of art, but I had a great time. I even began conducting my own art class there. For students I had a subway motorman—a dear old friend—an opera buff, and a sculptor who made things from railroad ties. They would come in day after day, and we would talk about art—their work and mine.

The Jazz Man was my first attempt at illustrating a children's book in woodcuts. I did the work for this book on old orange crates! Mother was inspired to write the book by a woodcut I had done of an African American musician.

The three other books I illustrated in woodcuts after *The Jazz Man* were *The Ballad of the Burglar of Babylon*, an exciting and dramatic poem written by the Pulitzer Prize winner Elizabeth

Bishop [Farrar, 1968]; *Don't You Turn Back: Poems by Langston Hughes*, selected by Lee Bennett Hopkins [Knopf, 1969]; and *David He No Fear*, an African Bible tale retold by Lorenz Graham [Crowell, 1971].

The Village of Round and Square Houses came about from a visit to Tos, a village unlike any other place in the world. It is in the remote hills of the Cameroons in Africa. I learned the story from a young woman who grew up there.

Blair Lent

Blair Lent, born on January 22, 1930, in Boston, Massachusetts, graduated from the Boston Museum School of Fine Arts in 1953, and began writing and illustrating children's books in 1964. One of the first books he illustrated, The Wave, *by Margaret Hodges (Houghton, 1964), is a Caldecott Honor Book. Other Caldecott Honor Books include* Why the Sun and the Moon Live in the Sky: An African Folktale *by Elphinstone Dayrell (Houghton, 1968), and* The Angry Moon, *by William Sleator (Atlantic, 1970). He received the Caldecott Medal for* The Funny Little Woman, *retold by Arlene Mosel (Dutton, 1972). He lives in Massachusetts.*

I was an only child living in a world peopled by imaginary friends. The friends were often first encountered in storybooks my father brought to me from secondhand bookstores.

It was during the Depression years, and my family could not afford new books.

My parents encouraged my early efforts at writing and illustrating stories, and my grandmother told me many of her own stories. She and I often collaborated on wild tales, and I knew then, as a small boy, that what I hoped to do with my life was to travel around the world and write about and draw pictures of my many adventures.

In 1953, after graduating from the Boston Museum School, I was awarded the Cummings Traveling Scholarship and spent a year studying in Switzerland and Italy.

After receiving a second traveling scholarship from the Museum, I went to the Soviet Union. I sketched old but rapidly modernizing villages; I traveled over the steppes, down the Don, through birch forests, and into Volga villages. I studied the fantastic wooden architecture of Kizhi and the kremlins of Novgorod, Zagorsk, Suzdal, Rostov, and Moscow. I talked with the art director of a children's book publishing house in Moscow and visited several painters, printmakers, and illustrators in many Soviet cities.

I had always wanted to do children's books. While working in an advertising agency, I kept writing and illustrating stories and submitting them to publishers. Finally, almost simultaneously, Walter Lorraine, an art director at Houghton, gave me the opportunity to illustrate *The Wave*, and Emilie McLeod, children's book editor at Atlantic, decided to publish *Pistachio* [1964], a story I both wrote and illustrated, that was inspired by a roadside circus performance I watched one evening in Paris on the banks of the Seine.

A technique I use in most of my work is printing from cardboard cuts. The results resemble a woodcut, but the surface of the cardboard is much easier to cut into. I can vary the texture by cutting into the cardboard to different depths. I can also use different methods of cutting, like pricking the surface of the cardboard with a pin or drawing with the edge of a razor blade. I make many prints of each illustration and then study the different prints and combine the most interesting parts from each. The collage made from the different prints is sent to the printer, who in turn reproduces the artwork on another printing surface from which the book itself is printed. I never see a finished illustration until after the book has been off the press. I used this technique with my first book, *The Wave*, and later with *Bayberry Bluff* [1987], and in *Molasses Flood* [1992; both Houghton].

I have very strong feelings about children's literature. Books were important to me as a child, and it is for that little boy that I am working. I can never know other children's innermost thoughts as well as I can remember my own.

Ed Emberley

Ed Emberley, born on October 19, 1931, in Maiden, Massachusetts, worked at a variety of jobs before doing his first book for children, The Wing on a Flea: A Book About Shapes *(Little, Brown, 1961). He received the Caldecott Medal for* Drummer Hoff *(1967), by his wife, Barbara, whom he met while attending the Massachusetts College of Arts in Boston. Their* One Wide River to Cross *(1966; both Prentice-Hall) is a Caldecott Honor Book. They live in Ipswich, Massachusetts.*

I had been waiting five years for a publisher to send me a book to illustrate. I finally decided that the most sensible way to convince an editor that I could indeed illustrate a children's book was to make one up, so I created *The Wing on a Flea*, with text and illustrations, along with a detailed dummy. It was accepted, published, and Barbara and I were off! When the book came out, I bought thirty copies of it and sent them to all the publishers I could think of with a letter asking them to consider my work for future books. Three publishing houses immediately accepted my offer. I've been doing children's books ever since.

With *Drummer Hoff*, Barbara and I wanted to do a picture book in which the pictures did most of the work. The thing that pleases us most in the book is the use of daisies and birds. They appear to be decorative elements all through the verses; then at the end you find that they are the point. They are the things that in the end survive and prosper. That's only one percent of the book; ninety-nine percent is a bright, colorful, decorative rendering of an old folk rhyme.

Barbara actively participates in almost all phases of our craft. For instance, over the years she has been involved in finding and adapting manuscripts, preparing worksheets for printers, preparing overlays for my master drawings, gathering material for future books, paying the bills, arranging for research trips, and taking most of the photographs we use.

Our work habits are simple. We do not work on Sunday, Thanksgiving, or Christmas. When our two children were younger, we did not work from the time school let out in the spring till the children went back to school in the fall. When doing artwork, Barbara and I work at adjoining tables; when working on anything to do with writing, we each have to be alone—absolutely and positively alone.

I have never worried about my audience. When in doubt, I do what I like as an adult. Children are individuals—there are always some who will like what I do. You can only talk to yourself and write to yourself and draw for yourself and for people just like you. It's only then that you can achieve depth. You start out to communicate with a handful of people, and that handful turns out to be millions.

Working in the field of children's books is challenging. It is a wonderful field to be involved in. It is one wide river to cross after another, and you never quite feel that you have reached the other side.

Nonny Hogrogian

Nonny Hogrogian, born on May 7, 1932, in the Bronx, New York, received the Caldecott Medal for Always Room for One More *by Sorche Nic Leodhas (Holt, 1965) and for* One Fine Day *(Macmillan, 1971). The Contest (Greenwillow, 1976) is a Caldecott Honor Book. She lives in Virginia with her husband, the writer David Kherdian.*

I attended public high school in the Bronx, and then went to study at Hunter College. I got through school by drawing. In the geography class, I made maps; in other classes I was appointed to such positions as chairman of the poster committee!

After graduating from Hunter College, I wanted to go into advertising work, but at the time women were not too welcome. I hated it, and so I took a job at William Morrow, the publishers, where I both designed and bought art for book jackets. From there I went to work at Crowell, where I met Elizabeth Riley. It was she who really gave me a start in illustrating books for children. I did the art for *King of the Kerry Fair* by Nicolette Meredith [Crowell] in 1960, but the excitement of the work did not come right away. It wasn't until I was saturated with Elizabeth Riley's well-used expression "The words come first" that I learned the true meaning of bookmaking. The manuscript does come first, and from that everything grows.

After working at Crowell I went to Holt and then on to Scribner's. It was there that I illustrated my first picture book, *Always Room for One More*. And, of all things, it won the Caldecott Medal! Winning the Caldecott changed my life completely. I was able to stop working and devote my full time to illustrating books for children.

Children's books should be as beautiful as they possibly can be. Kids grow up on picture books, and they should see beauty in them.

When I was young, my ability to draw felt like a gift. It was my joy, my companion, my ego builder, my time filler. It was my passport to life, and I used it and enjoyed using it.

Arnold Lobel

Arnold Lobel, born on May 22, 1933, in Los Angeles, California, grew up in Schenectady, New York. He received a B.F.A. degree from the Pratt Institute in Brooklyn, New York, in 1955, and married Anita Kempler, who was also an art student at Pratt. Beginning in 1961 he wrote and illustrated a number of award-winning volumes, including Frog and Toad Are Friends *(Harper, 1970) and* Hildilid's Night *by Cheli Durán Ryan (Macmillan, 1971), both Caldecott Honor Books.* Frog and Toad Together *(Harper, 1972) is a Newbery Honor Book.* Fables *(Harper, 1980) received the Caldecott Medal. He was also the recipient of the 1985 University of Southern Mississippi Medallion. He died in New York City on December 4, 1987.*

My parents had gone from Schenectady, New York, to Los Angeles to find their fortunes. Of course there were no fortunes to be found in 1933, so they returned to Schenectady and to an eventual divorce. There I lived through a rather unhappy childhood, until I finally escaped to college in my late teens.

My stories usually emerge out of a visual idea, a situation, or a sequence of situations that I think would be fun to draw. Sometimes the story pops into place in just the right way, but more often than not it is a struggle for me. I never try my ideas out on children—they should see the finished performance, not the rehearsal. A good illustrator should have a repertory of styles at his command, like an actor switching from one role to another.

Writing is not so very pleasant for me. My head is not always full of wonderful stories. I sit for days at a time with a pencil and a pad and nothing happens at all. When a story begins to take shape on the pages of my notebook, I become very happy and excited. I read it over and over again. When the story is the best I can write, I draw the pictures for the dessert.

It is pleasing to know that, every day, people out there in the great big world are sitting around reading and enjoying my books. I guess you can guess that I love making books for children.

Tomie dePaola

Tomie dePaola was born on September 15, 1934, in Meriden, Connecticut. After receiving a B.F.A. degree from the Pratt Institute in Brooklyn, New York, he began his art career designing Christmas cards and stage sets, and doing liturgical art. His first book for children, The Wonderful Dragon of Timlin *(Bobbs-Merrill), appeared in 1966. Since that date he has written or provided illustrations for more than a hundred books.* Strega Nona *(Prentice-Hall, 1975) is a Caldecott Honor Book. Recipient of the 1981 Kerlan Award, the 1983 Regina Medal, and the 1995 University of Southern Mississippi Medallion, he lives in New London, New Hampshire.*

Books have always been important to me. By the time I could hold a pencil, I knew what my life's work would be. I remember way back in the early 1940s, when I was a young child, a poster—which I believe was for Book Week—depicted a ship made of books. At least I remember it that way, sailing off to "faraway places" with loads of book characters—Alice, Jo March, Robinson Crusoe, Puss-in-Boots, Cinderella, you name 'em. I just can't imagine life without books.

One of the first questions I get asked by children and grown-ups is where do my ideas come from? I don't really know. I guess they ultimately come from inside myself. All my characters seem to be part of me, even Helga from *Helga's Diary* [Harcourt, 1977] and Strega Nona. But what releases these ideas and characters is still a mystery to me. It can be one of those "light-bulb situations" like in the comic strips, or sometimes just plain tedious coaxing. Whenever the idea or character is ready to pop out, I'd better be ready to grab it. Then it is just good, old-fashioned hard work to take the idea and make it work. No magic involved, just hard work, some luck, a good editor, and a lot of love on my part.

Once, while I was in Italy, I met Leo Lionni, which was a genuine thrill. Over dinner he lowered his voice and asked me, "Do you ever worry you won't have any more ideas?" It was wonderful to hear that fear, which many of us have, expressed. "Of course I do," I said. "But I have a trick. I always try to come up with new projects before I finish the one I'm working on." It is sort of like baking sourdough bread: You take a little dough to start your new batch. I have every intention of continuing to work, including illustrating other people's texts. And I want to grow! That's important to me as an artist. To grow as an artist so I can give the children my very best—that is the important thing.

Art, music, literature, poetry, painting, and sculpture are not luxuries. They are necessary to the soul. We can feed the intellect, but if we don't feed the soul as well, the intellect is going to starve to death.

The storyteller has always been an extremely important person in our culture. A good children's artist-author is the storyteller of a new era. Of today. And that is what I want to be more than anything else in the world.

Uri Shulevitz

Uri Shulevitz was born on February 27, 1935, in Warsaw, Poland, and came to the United States at the age of twenty-four. He studied painting at the Brooklyn Museum Art School, and illustrated Hebrew books for children. He received the Caldecott Medal for The Fool of the World and the Flying Ship, *retold by Arthur Ransome (1968);* The Treasure *(1979; both Farrar) is a Caldecott Honor Book.* Writing with Pictures: How to Write and Illustrate Children's Books *(Watson-Guptill, 1985), a book for adults, was a ten-year project. He divides his time between Upstate New York and New York City.*

I began drawing at the age of three. Drawing has always been with me. The encouragement of my parents, who were both talented, probably contributed to my early interest in drawing.

I was four years old during World War II when the Warsaw blitz occurred. I can remember standing in line for bread when suddenly flying shrapnel and smoke were all over the place. When the smoke cleared, many people were lying on the ground, dead or wounded. When I went home, a bomb fell into the stairwell of my apartment building. I had to walk down a long plank where the stairway had been. It was like walking through an abyss.

My family was forced to leave Warsaw. We traveled from country to country, finally ending up in Paris. In 1949 we moved to Israel. During the day I worked at many jobs. I was an apprentice at a rubber-stamp shop, a carpenter, and a dog-license clerk at Tel Aviv City Hall. At the age of eighteen I was the youngest member to participate in a drawing exhibition at the Museum of Tel Aviv.

After serving in the Israeli Army during the Sinai War in 1956, I came to New York City. I like it here and appreciate very much the possibilities the United States has offered me.

After illustrating Hebrew books, I made up a portfolio and took it to Harper. Ursula Nordstrom, the editor in chief, was in Europe. Susan Hirschman, an editor in the children's book department, looked at my work and liked it. When Ursula Nordstrom came back, both she and Susan suggested that I write a book of my own. I did not consider myself a writer, but

I tried anyway. After many trials, my first book, *The Moon in My Room* [Harper, 1963], was published. Writing, I came to realize, has less to do with language than one thinks. First one has to have something to say. This may come in pictures or in sounds, depending on one's inclinations, and not necessarily in words.

A common theme ran through three of my early books—that of a child traveling outside his room without ever really leaving it. This theme ranged from total fantasy in *The Moon in My Room* to a confrontation between fantasy and reality in *One Monday Morning* [Scribner's, 1967], to a total reality in *Rain Rain River* [Farrar, 1969]. It was a long trip!

I love doing picture books. I like writing brief things. I basically do what I believe in, what I like, what I truly respond to. And I think that the only allowance one has to make for children is to write as simply as possible.

Illustrators

The picture book is a place where word and image meet.
—Lynd Ward

An illustrator's task is to interpret and transform the written word into something that must be seen to be experienced. Using materials such as crayons, chalk or charcoal, pencil, paint, or pen, these masters of their craft bring life to authors' words, producing visual portraits that enhance the simplest or the most sophisticated language.

Dorothy P. Lathrop

Dorothy P. Lathrop, born on April 16, 1891, in Albany, New York, had the distinction of being the first illustrator to receive the Caldecott Medal for Animals of the Bible: A Picture Book, *with text selected by Helen Dean Fisher from the King James Bible (Lippincott, 1937). Before that she provided the illustrations for the Newbery Medal winner* Hitty: Her First Hundred Years *by Rachel Field (1929). The Fairy Circus (1931), which she both wrote and illustrated, was named a Newbery Honor Book (both Macmillan). She died on December 30, 1980, in Falls Village, Connecticut.*

I grew up in an active, creative household. My mother, I. Pulis Lathrop, was an exhibiting painter; my sister, Gertrude, a sculptor. I became interested in books through my paternal grandfather, who owned a bookstore in Bridgeport, Connecticut.

After high school I attended Teachers College at Columbia University, and later the Pennsylvania Academy of Fine Arts. I decided to illustrate books for young children simply because I liked them. I began to illustrate in 1918, while I was teaching art in the Albany High School. One day at lunch a fellow teacher and I were looking at an illustrated book. I said, "I wish I could draw like that. I may not be a Howard Pyle, but I *want* to illustrate."

My first drawings were for a book called *Japanese Prints* by John Gould Fletcher [Four Seasons, 1919]. The company went bankrupt before they could pay me for my drawings!

It never occurred to me to make a book of the animal stories of the Bible. It was Helen Dean Fisher who for several years cherished that plan in secret, and when she chose me to illustrate it, I was very proud.

I don't know where my ideas come from. They develop as I work. Do I rework material? Of course! Do I try out my ideas on children? Never!

Feodor Rojankovsky

Feodor Rojankovsky was born on December 24, 1891, in Jelgava, Russia (now Latvia), on the shores of the Baltic Sea, where his father was the headmaster of a boys' high school. A year later his family moved to Revel (now Tallinn, Estonia); his childhood was divided between Tallinn and St. Petersburg. In 1941, after the German occupation of Paris, he immigrated to the United States. He received the Caldecott Medal for Frog Went A-Courtin', *retold by John Langstaff (Harcourt, 1955). He died on October 12, 1970, in New York.*

Three events influenced my becoming an artist. First, my father read to the family very often. Among his favorite books there were two that I could look at forever, the Bible and *Paradise Lost* by Milton, both illustrated by Gustave Doré.

A second event was when my father took me to a small zoo, where I saw the most marvelous creatures on earth. The third event was my receiving a set of colored pencils. The zoo became the favorite subject of my pictures, but the colored pencils were used up before my elephant looked anything like an elephant!

One Christmas in St. Petersburg, I received *Robinson Crusoe* by Daniel Defoe, in a Russian translation that impressed me very deeply. It was the first book that I started illustrating. I was eight or nine years old at the time and remember that I felt the island and the house of Robinson Crusoe were not well enough represented in the illustrations. I remember how hard I tried to "enrich" it!

In 1912 I entered the Moscow Academy of Fine Arts. I was happy to be living in the town where the Stanislavsky theater was founded, where Chekhov lived, and where Tolstoy often visited: Serov, Vroubel, Korovine lived in Moscow, also. Two of them were teaching in the Fine Arts Academy. Here I also met the great poet Mayakovsky, a pupil of our school. Mayakovsky called me the "Frenchman" because of my paintings on a given subject. I was at the time under the influence of Gauguin, Matisse, and Marquet.

From 1914 to 1917 I served as an officer in the Russian army. During this time I was badly wounded and began to paint war subjects from memory while I was recuperating. The sketches I did became my first published works. In 1919 I was mobilized by the White Army, and soon my military service was ended behind barbed wire in Poland. After I left Poland, I went to Berlin and finally to Paris. In Paris I met my first American publishers, Esther Averill and Lila Stanley, who were organizers of the

Domino Press. I did *Daniel Boone* for them, which was published in 1931.

A good children's book is one that has a good text full of action but is not sophisticated, one that tells the child the truth like a tale, and a tale like the truth!

Symeon Shimin

Symeon Shimin, born on November 1, 1902, in Astrakhan, on the Volga River in Russia, came to the United States at the age of nine. In 1938 he was chosen to paint a mural in the Department of Justice Building in Washington, D.C. Since then his works have been exhibited in major museums in the United States and Canada. An accomplished self-taught painter, he entered the field of children's books in 1950, illustrating works by such well-known authors as Madeleine L'Engle and Virginia Hamilton. He lives in New York City.

For years, after coming to America, our big family lived in two tiny rooms at the rear of my parents' delicatessen store. After school and during the summer I worked in the store.

I never drew as a child. My heart was in music, and I wanted to become a musician. I never thought about drawing. I didn't know what a *painter* meant nor what *painting* meant.

Then one day—the next day or the next week of my childhood, it seems—I drew. And I have never stopped drawing.

During my teens I did some freelance advertising work, making just enough money to live on. At twenty I fought a serious bout with tuberculosis, which limited my working to an hour or so a day; even so, I was able to earn my keep doing artwork.

Managing to get to Europe, I spent a year and a half studying the work of El Greco, Cézanne, and Picasso in museums and art galleries. This served as my art training.

When I came back to America, I found myself in the beginning of the Depression. In the late 1930s a national competition was held for artists under Franklin Delano Roosevelt's administration. I planned to enter the competition and do a mural for the United States Department of Justice Building. I worked on several ideas, but the day before the final sketches were due in Washington, I decided to do something entirely different. I phoned Washington and asked if the committee would accept a drawing delivered in person rather than by mail. When they told me they would, I went to work, finished a sketch, boarded a train in the middle of the night from New York to Washington, and slipped it under a door!

One week later I found out that I was the winner in the competition. This led to several successful one-man shows.

Good friends of mine, Herman and Nina Schneider, a well-known team of writers who did science books for children, encouraged me to illustrate a revised edition of their book *How Big Is Big?* [Scott, 1950]. I did it, and that was the start of it all!

I don't work steadily at book illustration. I illustrate for a time and then stop to paint. In doing book illustrations I always use live models. I do dozens of drawings from each sketch until I feel the illustrations are perfect. I work in watercolor and in acrylics.

Art means everything to me. It is my life. It is *me*!

Louis Slobodkin

Louis Slobodkin, born on February 19, 1903, in Albany, New York, was one of America's foremost sculptors before he began illustrating books for children. The first book he illustrated was The Moffats *(1941) by Eleanor Estes. He provided illustrations for other books by Estes, including her three Newbery Honor Books,* The Middle Moffat *(1942),* Rufus M. *(1943), and* The Hundred Dresses *(1944). He received the Caldecott Medal for* Many Moons *by James Thurber (1943; all Harcourt). He died on May 8, 1975, in Miami Beach, Florida.*

When I discovered I could draw, I decided to become an artist. Someone gave me a few pounds of modeling clay when I was thirteen, so I became a sculptor.

At the age of fifteen, during my third year at high school, I decided to quit school and study art. I forced my parents' permission by instigating the first one-man sit-down strike

I'd ever heard of. I would attend class at the high school, but would refuse to do any work. After enough zeroes piled up, I was allowed to leave school. I worked that spring and summer bellhopping at a hotel and earned enough money to take me to New York City the following October. I registered at the Beaux Arts Institute of Design and studied in the life-modeling and drawing classes for the next five years. I took time out during the spring and summer to earn money as a factory hand, waiter, dishwasher, or the like, just to keep me going.

I did a great deal of sculpting. Probably my best-known public work is the eight-foot bronze statue of Abraham Lincoln, resting on a block of black Virginia granite, which stands in the Department of the Interior Building in Washington, D.C.; it was originally designed and executed for the 1939 New York World's Fair.

I might have devoted myself more to sculpture and less to books had I not had two very fortunate "accidents"; one was meeting Eleanor Estes, the other winning the Caldecott Award. After illustrating *The Moffats*, I was hooked on children's books and have worked on them since that time.

When I did *Many Moons*, I had no relationship with James Thurber whatsoever. Our collaboration was handled entirely by the publishers, and I was not allowed to push any words around in his manuscript, as I usually did when I collaborated on a book. I remember the shock that shook the publishing house when I wanted to change one word in Mr. Thurber's manuscript; I wanted to say "The moon is made of *blue* cheese" instead of "*green* cheese." My reason was that in printing the book there was no provision for yellow on that particular page. I only had red and blue. Anyone knows you need yellow and blue to make *green*!

Great art has many facets. It is composed of countless esthetic truths. An artist's personal style develops when he realizes that there are certain art facets he sees and feels more clearly than all others. His style is his own emphasis on those esthetic truths he feels most strongly, and he uses his medium to shout or whisper his concern with those truths. If his interpretation is deeply and honestly felt, his art mirrors his strong individuality. And that is the main quality; that is the voice that differentiates him from the babble around him.

Lynd Ward

Lynd Ward was born on June 26, 1905, in Chicago, Illinois, the son of a Methodist minister, and spent his childhood years in Illinois, Massachusetts, and New Jersey. He graduated from Teachers College, Columbia University, in New York City, in 1926. He married May McNeer, and in 1929 they collaborated on Prince Bantam *(Macmillan), the first of many titles they produced together.* America's Ethan Allen *by Stewart Holbrook (1949) is a Caldecott Honor Book; he received the Caldecott Medal for* The Biggest Bear *(1952; both Houghton). Among his many awards are the 1973 University of Southern Mississippi Medallion and the 1975 Regina Medal (corecipient with May McNeer). He was an accomplished artist whose paintings are in the permanent collections of the Library of Congress, the Smithsonian Institution, and the Metropolitan Museum of Art. He died on June 28, 1985, in Reston, Virginia.*

I began drawing when I discovered that WARD was DRAW spelled backward! I became interested in children's books while studying at Teachers College at Columbia. I decided that books, illustrating, and graphic arts were fields that interested me most.

The Biggest Bear came about quite naturally. Each year since my childhood, I had spent summers at Lonely Lake in the backwoods of Canada, a remote area in Ontario. I often saw bear cubs tied up as pets, at nearby farms. I decided to use opaque watercolors to depict the Canadian countryside, an area I loved so much.

Most of my time is spent on illustration. I do not consider myself a writer but rather an artist whose stories sometimes need some words. *The Biggest Bear* was finished completely as a sequence of pictures. Then a minimum of words were added to hold it together. What little I know about writing is due to living and working with a fine and sensitive writer—my wife.

The picture book is a place where word and image meet and the interrelation between the two is of necessity the primary concern of the exploring artist. For the artist there is the stimulation of a multitude of ideas, the encounter with other minds, and the constant challenge of technical problems that are so rarely completely solved. We recognize, I think, that no earlier generation of artists has had so much variety in getting a picture onto a book page, and the result has been a richness of expression, particularly in books for children. Their needs impose an especially great responsibility on us, and in that perspective I have always believed that our best is the least we should come up with.

The artist must be concerned with what he does, because what he is doing is really communicating—and this has something to do with what the world is going to be like in the years ahead.

The artist must grow so that what he does today is better than what he did yesterday, and what he does tomorrow will, by the grace of God, be an advance over both.

Paul Galdone

Paul Galdone, born in 1907 in Budapest, Hungary, came to the United States in 1921. A job in the art department at Doubleday led to his designing book jackets and eventually illustrating many books. Anatole *(1956) and* Anatole and the Cat *(1957; both McGraw-Hill) by Eve Titus are Caldecott Honor Books. He died on November 7, 1986, in Nyack, New York.* The Complete Story of the Three Blind Mice *by John W. Irving (Clarion, 1987) was published posthumously.*

When my family left Budapest, we arrived in New Jersey, where I was promptly enrolled in high school. The Hungarian language did not prove very useful in the United States.

In an effort to get me over the barrier, I had to attend three English classes every day in addition to a biology class. When it came my turn to read from Shakespeare's *Midsummer Night's Dream*, I was highly embarrassed. Not only did I have an accent that amused the whole class, but I also failed to understand most of what I was trying to read. In the biology class, however, I felt more successful; when it was discovered that I was proficient in the drawing of grasshoppers, I was soon drawing them for all the other pupils!

Shortly afterward we moved to New York City. To help support my family in the struggle to get started, I worked during the day as a busboy, an electrician's helper on unfinished skyscrapers, a fur dryer, and more! At night I attended art schools: the Art Students League and the New York School for Industrial Design. Eventually, four years of working in the art department at Doubleday determined my life's direction. I loved everything in the world of book production—the people and the challenges. There I had a chance to design my first book jacket. That all led into my freelancing as a book-jacket designer.

I lived in Greenwich Village, and while I freelanced and built up a busy career in book-jacket designing, I kept up my interest in fine arts by drawing and painting and by long sketching vacations in Vermont. I also became increasingly interested in book illustration. After four years in the United States Army Engineer Corps, during which I contributed to *Yank Magazine* in my spare time, I settled down in Rockland County, New York—with a wife, and eventually two children and assorted animals—and resumed freelancing, leaning more and more toward illustrating children's books.

Leo Politi

Leo Politi, born on November 21, 1908, in Fresno, California, returned at the age of seven to his mother's childhood home in Brani, a town near Milan in northern Italy where he lived for seventeen years. At fifteen he received a scholarship to study at the Art Institute at the Royal Palace of Monza near Milan and graduated as an art teacher. Returning to the United States, he published his first book, Little Pancho *(Viking, 1938).* Pedro, the Angel of Olvera Street *(1946) and* Juanita *(1948) are Caldecott Honor Books.* Song of the Swallows *(1949; all Scribner's) received the Caldecott Medal. Recipient of the 1966 Regina Medal, he lives in Los Angeles, California, where an elementary school is named in his honor.*

*P*edro, the Angel of Olvera Street, about a famous Mexican celebration on Olvera Street in Los Angeles, was inspired by my editor, Alice Dalgliesh at Scribner's. I had sent her a Christmas card with a little red-winged Mexican angel. She wrote to me saying that I should make a book about this lovely angel. *Pedro* is my favorite book because I put more work in it than any of the books I have done. It was the result of many years of drawing on Olvera Street, a street where I lived and worked when I returned from Italy.

Song of the Swallows was also suggested by Alice Dalgliesh. When she asked if I would like to do the book, I was very enthusiastic because I like the Mission of Capistrano so well. The fact that the swallows return punctually every spring is to me such a sweet and poetic happening. But I have been interested in swallows ever since I was a boy in Italy, where two swallows came to nest every spring under the roof beams of my grandfather's house. I remember all the joy they brought. I used to like to watch them and was always impressed by their elegance in flight.

When I went to the mission, I learned that an old gardener named Julian had lived in the mission all his life and had recently died. Julian became one of the main characters in the book. As for Juan, I could picture the hundreds of boys and girls like him who, on their way to and from school, stopped to talk with Julian and listened to the stories of flowers, of birds, and of the Mission of San Juan Capistrano. Winning the Caldecott Award for this book sort of gave me assurance that I was doing the right things for children. I felt very grateful and fortunate. It was like a stimulant to better my work, which I believe is the primary goal of life.

I had no training in writing, and naturally I find writing more difficult to do than illustrating. I work and rework my material up to the very last day of my deadline. I have never tried out ideas on children. I do ask opinions of adults, especially from those with good taste. They can help a lot.

I love children—all children! Each of them has the capacity to become a good artist, a good architect, or a good scientist, or to succeed in any other human endeavor. If children work at it, there is no limit to what they can accomplish.

Evaline Ness

Evaline Ness, born on April 24, 1911, in Union City, Ohio, grew up in Pontiac, Michigan. Before illustrating books for children, she had a successful career in fashion design, which involved a great deal of travel throughout the world. She was married to Eliot Ness, the F.B.I. agent of "Untouchable" fame. After illustrating many books and designing scores of book jackets, she wrote and illustrated Josefina February *(Scribner's, 1963). Three books that she illustrated are Caldecott Honor Books:* All in the Morning Early *by Sorche Nic Leodhas (1963),* A Pocketful of Cricket *by Rebecca Caudill (1964; both Holt), and* Tom Tit Tot *by Joseph Jacobs (Scribner's, 1965). She received the Caldecott Medal for* Sam, Bangs & Moonshine, *which she both wrote and illustrated (Holt, 1966). She died on August 12, 1986, in Kingston, New York.*

After attending one year at Muncie State Teachers College in Muncie, Indiana, I decided that I wanted to be an artist more than anything else, so I went to the Chicago Art Institute for two years, where I got my first big break. I did a whole page of fashion drawings for a large department store, Carson Pirie Scott, that appeared in the *Chicago Tribune*. It was then that I decided I would take this little triumph to New York, where I had always wanted to live anyway. And so I did!

When I came to New York in 1946, I began illustrating for the magazine *Seventeen*; this led to fashion drawing for the Saks Fifth Avenue department store.

I started illustrating children's books at the suggestion of Mary Cosgrove, editor of children's books at Houghton Mifflin. My first, *The Bridge* by Charlton Ogburn, Jr., came out in 1957. I loved the book.

The first book I attempted to both write and illustrate, *Josefina February*, developed at the suggestion of Nancy Quint, who was children's book editor at Scribner's. Nancy saw some large woodcuts I had made after a year's stay in Haiti and simply said, "Why don't you write a story?" After a lot of simpering and protestations that I wasn't a writer, I wrote the story *around* the pictures. This is something I never did again. The only thing that comes close to that experience was that Sam in *Sam, Bangs & Moonshine* was a drawing fait accompli; one of the many I had kept in a portfolio of drawings I was always doing and which I kept strictly for myself.

Sam, Bangs & Moonshine was also a result of prodding, this time by Ann Durrell, who was an editor at Holt, Rinehart, and Winston. Ann and I talked through lunch one day, and all afternoon at my apartment, about things we could remember as children. I always leaned toward the child with faults—is there any other kind except in people's imaginations? I decided Sam would be a liar, the same kind *I* was when *I* was a child, except that I made up new lies for her to tell.

My favorite book is always my last one because I am always dissatisfied with the ones that have come before—regardless of the attention they have received.

Nicolas Mordvinoff

Nicolas Mordvinoff, who often published under the name Nicolas, was born on September 27, 1911, in St. Petersburg, Russia. After the Russian Revolution his family fled via Finland to Paris, France. There he studied art at both the Lycée Jeanson de Sailly and the École des Roches, before graduating from the University of Paris with a degree in Latin, philosophy, and languages. The first book he illustrated, Thunder Island *by William S. Stone (Knopf, 1942), was published while he was living in Tahiti. He came to the United States in 1946. Two of the many books he illustrated by Will (Lipkind) are* The Two Reds *(1950), a Caldecott Honor Book, and* Finders Keepers *(1951; both Harcourt), which received the Caldecott Medal. In addition to being an illustrator, he was a noted painter and graphic artist, and his works are in the permanent collection of the Metropolitan Museum of Art in New York City. He signed many of his paintings under the pseudonyms Fernand Leger and Anedée Ozenfant. He died on May 5, 1973, in Hampton, New Jersey.*

Although Paris in the 1930s was gay, vibrant, and experiencing a cultural explosion, I felt the need to escape the pace, to find myself. For the next thirteen years I lived in the South Pacific, traveling from island to island, painting, developing a style of my own.

While I was living in Tahiti, World War II broke out. I wanted desperately to fight in the war, but I couldn't get into an army.

The French wouldn't take me, the Russians wouldn't take me, and neither would the United States.

The natives bought my paintings. They called them photographs, and paid me in pearls. One day a chief came to me and asked if I would make a photograph of his wife. I told him I would and asked if I could meet her. "She's dead," he replied. However, he did have a poor photograph that had been taken of her by a visitor some time ago.

I did a portrait painting from the photograph, and when it was ready, the chief came to my studio. I put it on the easel. The chief sat down, looked at it carefully, walked up to it, touched it, and said, "She's alive again!" He pulled out a huge, beautifully colored pearl to pay me for the portrait. It was the biggest pearl I had ever seen in my entire life.

In Tahiti I met William S. Stone, who was finishing a manuscript. He persuaded me to do the illustrations for *Thunder Island*. After it was published, I did two other books with him; the work made me believe I would be successful in the United States.

In 1946 I settled in New York City. This was a terrible experience. I couldn't find a job, and I had no money. For one year I starved. A kindly editor sent me a box of chocolates. Chocolates! Better she should have sent a ham or a cheese. But chocolates!

About this time I met Maria Cimino of the New York Public Library, the wife of Will Lipkind. Will, an anthropologist by profession and a poet by inclination, talked to me about doing a book together. I saw a red cat on the windowsill and said, "Let's do a book about that cat." Will told me we needed more for a story. Returning from shopping that same night, I saw a boy with red hair. So *The Two Reds*, the cat and the boy, became the book.

Winning the Caldecott Medal for *Finders Keepers* was everything to me. It changed my whole life. Instead of going hungry with my samples under my arms and holes in the soles of my shoes, I had to fight editors off the telephone!

Will and I did many, many books together. The last one we did was *The Boy and the Forest* [Harcourt, 1964]. After I finished it, I decided to stop doing children's books. It was an interlude in my life.

I returned to painting.

Garth Williams

Garth Williams was born on April 16, 1912, in New York City. He has created his own books for children, including his first, The Chicken Book *(Howell, Soskin, 1946; reissued by Delacorte, 1990). His illustrations have also embellished a host of classic works, including* Stuart Little *(1945) and* Charlotte's Web *(1952) by E. B. White, and the Little House series by Laura Ingalls Wilder (all Harper). He lives in San Antonio, Texas.*

My mother says I was born on the fifteenth of April in 1912. The news of the sinking of the *Titanic* arrived at the same time I did, and was so sensational that they didn't get around to registering me officially until April 16!

I grew up in a variety of places and countries. I was taken to Europe very early in my life to be shown off to my relations. I spoke French first, so my mother told me. But I was soon back in the wilds of Caldwell, New Jersey. I recall being taken to Canada at the age of six, and when I was ten, I was taken to England to be schooled. There I became the English schoolboy. Tom Brown's school days were very much like my own.

It was at the time of the Depression that I had to select a college for a profession. I had decided at the age of ten that I would become an architect. But by the time I was eighteen, the future for an architect was hopeless, so off I went to art school. My parents were both artists. My father, at sixteen, had sold two drawings to *Punch*, the British humor magazine; Mother was a painter. I studied painting and sculpture, theatrical design, and advertising; I was a principal of an art school for a year; then I won the British Prix de Rome for sculpture and went to Rome. I returned to London just before Britain declared war in 1939.

In 1943 I went to Harper with a portfolio of paintings, photographs of sculpture and architectural projects, cartoons, caricatures, fabric designs, murals, and portrait drawings. Ursula Nordstrom, the editor of children's books, said she had a manuscript coming in shortly which I could perhaps try to illustrate. The manuscript was *Stuart Little*.

I first met E. B. White a few days after reading the manuscript. He struck me as shy, and after talking for a while he asked, "Do you like my story?" This seemed strange to me, as I had thought the story was just wonderful and would have illustrated it for the sheer pleasure.

In *Stuart Little* E. B. White wanted me to illustrate the old double-decker Fifth Avenue bus of that period. I made the drawings in pencil first. These were sent to him, and he scribbled any comments he wished to in the margin. The drawings then came back to me, and I inked them in. His comments were always encouraging.

Seven years later we teamed up again to do *Charlotte's Web*. But I found *Stuart Little* more fun to illustrate than *Charlotte's Web* as there were more moments of fantasy in it. In *Charlotte's Web* I had to keep from disturbing the dull and ordinary background of the family so that the contrast of the animals' lives would be kept as in the text.

Stuart Little and *Charlotte's Web*, of course, are among my personal favorites. I feel extremely lucky to be able to share a little of the spotlight of these two books—books I love, admire, envy, and emulate as an author.

The Little House series took me several years just to do the research and three years to do the many pictures for the eight books. I visited Laura Ingalls Wilder at her home in Mansfield, Missouri, in 1947; she was eighty years old at the time. I stood watching her for a while when I drove up to her house. She was sprightly and cheerful, working in her garden. I met with her and her husband, Almanzo, with a list of questions to ask about their lives. She told me where to find all the "little houses" where she had lived. Later, I drove to all the sites. We found where the little house on the prairie was, traveled to the banks of Plum Creek in Minnesota. In De Smet, South Dakota, I met people who knew the Ingalls family and found their farm. I took many photographs and made many sketches.

The life of an illustrator is very pleasant, so I have remained one. It has been a wonderful life even with all the disappointments. I am still illustrating and may be doing so until I am ninety—or more—and that's only a tomorrow away!

Marc Simont

Marc Simont, born on November 23, 1915, in Paris, France, traveled widely before permanently settling in the United States in the mid-1930s. He worked as a teacher, portrait painter, illustrator, and muralist before beginning to illustrate books for children in the early 1940s. The Happy Day *by Ruth Krauss (1949) is a Caldecott Honor Book; he received the Caldecott Medal for* A Tree Is Nice *by Janice May Udry (1956; both Harper). In 1990* The 13 Clocks *and* The Wonderful O *by James Thurber, which he illustrated in the 1950s, were reissued by Donald I. Fine, Inc. He lives in West Cornwall, Connecticut.*

The first twenty years of my life were spent shuttling back and forth between France, Spain, and the United States, seldom staying longer than five years in any one place. Like any child I drew pictures, but unlike a lot of children, I never stopped. I was fortunate enough to have an artist right in my house, my father, José, who worked for thirty years on the staff of the magazine *L'Illustration* and who taught me to handle the tools of the trade. He was always my most important teacher.

When I came to the United States in the 1930s, I took whatever jobs I could find before I began to get professional work. I was lucky to break into the field of illustrating books for children.

In *A Tree Is Nice*, Janice May Udry gave me everything an artist could want in a picture-book manuscript. The idea of *A Tree Is Nice* is so fundamental and uncluttered that when I first read it, I said to myself, "Now, why didn't I think of that?" The manuscript had a solid, basic idea presented with simplicity and charm; all I had to do was keep pace with it.

I believe that if I like the drawings I do, children will like them also. The child in me must make contact with other children. I may miss it by ten miles, but if I am going to hit, it's because of the child in me. Actually, with my work I don't know if I'm pleased until it's all over!

Leonard Weisgard

Leonard Weisgard, born on December 13, 1916, in New Haven, Connecticut, studied at the Pratt Institute and the New School for Social Research in New York City. He has been illustrating books for children since 1937. Little Lost Lamb *by Golden MacDonald, a pseudonym of Margaret Wise Brown (Doubleday, 1945), and* Rain Drop Splash *by Alvin Tresselt (Lothrop, 1946) are*

Caldecott Honor Books. He received the Caldecott Medal for The Little Island *by Golden MacDonald (Doubleday, 1946). In 1953 he designed the sets and costumes for the first full-length American production of Tchaikovsky's* The Nutcracker. *He lives in Roxbury, Connecticut.*

I attended the New York City public schools for a number of years. A teacher in the lower grades inaugurated an art squad after school, which inspired my interest in drawing and painting. Another teacher introduced me to the theater. And the excitement of friends who believed in what they were doing encouraged me. My parents were usually aghast at what I was doing, and my interest in modern dance puzzled all!

I decided to illustrate books for children because most books I had seen for young people were so dreadful. My friends, who felt deeply about books, art, and the state of the world in the 1930s, felt we could do better. Because of the books that inspired us, we felt we, too, could move young people's books forward and give a needed sense of involvement between the child and books.

The Noisy Books grew out of a real need for excitement and provocative material for the very young. The first, *The Noisy Book*, was published by W. R. Scott, in 1939. Almost each year for the next decade, Margaret Wise Brown and I did another. Harper has now reissued the books.

Different books had different reasons for their birth and conception; some pleased me more than others. Illustrating *The Secret River* by Marjorie Kinnan Rawlings [Scribner's, 1955], a book that received a Newbery Honor, was indeed a challenge, for here was a book telling a story about a different child, and Marjorie told it so well that no one realized the child was a deprived, dark-skinned girl poet.

I wonder a great deal. I wonder mightily about our educational process and do believe we learn far more than we ever realize from people outside of schools, from those we love, respect, and admire, and sometimes a great deal from those we intensely dislike. Do we learn more standing still in one place or moving about a great deal? How do we learn? May Garelick shrewdly asked *Where Does the Butterfly Go When It Rains.* Sometimes not knowing a specific answer can be most provocative.

A child usually finds an answer before he even asks; he goes to books for answers to questions that are perennially a mystery to us. I respect and admire the potential of children more than anything else. Their intelligence and sensitivity amaze and delight me, and they make us humans who believe we may be adult seem foolish. I like to believe I am a human being concerned with all human beings and creatures alive on this earth.

Marcia Brown

Marcia Brown, born on July 13, 1918, in Rochester, New York, studied painting at the Woodstock School of Painting, the New School for Social Research, and the Art Students League. She is the only illustrator in the history of the Caldecott Awards to receive three Caldecott Medals: for Cinderella, or the Little Glass Slipper, *by Charles Perrault (1954), for* Once a Mouse . . . *which she wrote and illustrated (1961), and for* Shadow, *translated from the French of Blaise Cendrars (1982). Six of her books are Caldecott Honor Books:* Stone Soup: An Old Tale *(1947),* Henry-Fisherman: A Story of the Virgin Islands *(1949),* Dick Whittington and His Cat *(1950),* Skipper John's Cook *(1951), all of which she wrote and illustrated,* Puss in Boots *by Charles Perrault (1952), and* The Steadfast Tin Soldier *by Hans Christian Andersen (1953; all Scribner's). Her many awards and honors include the 1977 Regina Medal, the 1972 University of Southern Mississippi Medallion, and the 1992 Laura Ingalls Wilder Award. She lives in Connecticut.*

My interest in making picture books comes in an almost unbroken line from the constant reading and drawing of my childhood. Pictures popped into my head as I read, and I read voraciously. Every Christmas, my sister and I received paints and crayons and large pads of drawing paper. Christmas morning would find us making paper dolls and painting pictures of sturdy red barns with angels or fairies hovering overhead. Sometimes Mother and Father joined us, for drawing seemed most natural for the whole family to do. We all loved to read and listen to stories.

Because my father was a minister, we moved around. Each time we did, I would seek out the nearest public library and obtain a library card before my parents had finished unpacking their belongings.

My first four books were finished while I was working in the New York Public Library. I prepared exhibitions for five years in the rare-book collection, and also told stories to children. I went to playgrounds and recreation areas all over the city to do storytelling. I left library work in 1948 to devote my time to doing books.

My first book, *The Little Carousel*, was published by Scribner's in 1946. At that time I lived in the middle of a Sicilian neighborhood on Sullivan Street in New York's Greenwich Village. From my apartment window I saw the little street carousel arrive, and the episode that makes the plot of the story happened before my delighted eyes.

I had heard Alice Dalgliesh speak and admired the Scribner's list, so I made my way to Alice's office. Alice, who later became a very dear friend of mine, was too busy to see me. I burst into tears. I left the office and walked around the corner to Viking. But there I found Viking tied up with an elevator strike, and Miss Massee's office was on a high floor! So, rather than climb, I decided to wait for Miss Dalgliesh, who took the book.

The need for a variety in my books is a matter of temperament. I could no more stand using the same style art in book after book than I could eating the same food every day—and I love food and eat everything!

Books are to me as individual as people are, and I feel if a book is to be a unique experience for the child looking at it, it draws on a unique set of feelings in you before you make it.

When I finish a book, I am anxious to forget it so that I can free myself of its atmosphere and clear out all my impressions to try to make way for the next one.

Beni Montresor

Beni Montresor was born on March 31, 1926, in Bussolengo, near Verona, Italy. He has designed sets and costumes for New York, Hollywood, and European productions of Broadway plays, film productions, and operas. He came to the United States in 1960, when he began illustrating books for children. He received the Caldecott Medal for May I Bring a Friend? *by Beatrice Schenk de Regniers (Atheneum, 1964). In 1966 he was knighted by the Italian government for services to the arts, which gives him the title Cavaliere. He divides his time between New York City and Europe.*

I think I was born with a pencil in my hand. I vividly recall my grandfather going to Verona each Friday, returning home with toys and cake for me. I remember one day I said to my grandfather, "Next time you go to Verona, bring me some colored pencils instead of cake, because I want to draw pictures." The following Friday my grandfather came back from Verona with a new kind of present. And from that moment Verona became a magic place where you bought the colored pencils needed by a three-year-old painter.

When I asked my parents if I could go to high school in Verona, they were perplexed. The idea of having a young man study at the High School of Arts, and having an artist in the family, astounded them. Their idea of an artist was a loose-living pauper with too many nude models around. But help came unexpectedly from our country priest, and so I was enrolled at the art school.

While I was there, the war broke out. One morning I looked out the window and saw airplanes flying over Verona. Seconds later bombs fell on the city. I was fourteen years old at the time. I remember corpses lined up along the sidewalks covered with dirt and rubble and tiny pieces of flesh strewn in the streets.

I continued to go to school even during the bombardments. Little by little Verona was completely disfigured and seemed like one huge, tottering building in the course of demolition.

When the war was nearly over at last, and I had become so numbed by terror that I seemed like a wooden statue of a boy, the Nazis left, blowing up all the beautiful old bridges of Verona. It is impossible to explain how terrible things were in this beautiful city. Even today, after all this time, if I hear talk of war I freeze up into that wooden statue of a boy who lived in Verona during the bombardments.

When I came to New York City in 1960, on a Christmas vacation, I saw the city, and it was love at first sight. New York City is the moon; it is almost unreal.

It was in New York that someone suggested I illustrate a children's book. I wasn't too sure about this. I didn't have books as a child. I didn't know what to do, but I did it!

My pictures and work, I'm told, reflect an attitude about life that is optimistic. If they do, it is because I'm an optimist, and I believe that life, essentially, is very beautiful. It is bad only when you refuse to make the best of living.

Tom Feelings

Tom Feelings, born on May 19, 1933, in Brooklyn, New York, spent many years working in Africa after attending the School of Visual Arts in New York City. The first book he illustrated for children, Bola and the Oba's Drummers *by Letta Schatz (McGraw-Hill), appeared in 1967.* To Be a Slave *by Julius Lester (1968) is a Newbery Honor Book;* Moja Means One: Swahili Counting Book *(1971) and* Jambo Means Hello: Swahili Alphabet Book *(1974), both by Muriel Feelings, are Caldecott Honor Books. He twice received the Coretta Scott King Award: for* Something on My Mind *by Nikki Grimes (1978), and for* Soul Looks Back in Wonder *(1993; all Dial), a collection of poems by African American writers, illustrated in full-color paintings, which marked his debut as an anthologist. He lives in Columbia, South Carolina.*

During the mid-1960s I worked in West Africa, in Ghana, for the Ghana Publishing Company. There I illustrated the magazine *African Review* and also worked on syndicated newspapers, booklets, educational materials, and visual materials for both Ghana television and the Ghana airport. Ghana was my first lesson and experience with "black power"; my initial impressions were those of pride in seeing every facet of life manned by blacks—banks, industries, schools, the mass media including press, radio, and television. It was an inspiration to work for a black establishment, something I had never before had the opportunity to do. I was not asked, "Why are you drawing black people?" as I was functioning in an all-black country.

One day when looking through the work I had done in Brooklyn, an African artist in Ghana asked me, "Why do the black children that you draw always look so sad?" I had never thought of their expressions as sad when I was in the United States. I soon saw why they looked so to him. African children are basically happy, stable, and secure children, and this well-being is reflected in their glowing faces. I discovered this as I began to look at and draw them. This was one of the beautiful experiences I gained in Africa. Another thing that influenced my work was the colors. I began to depict these colors in scenes showing the dress and outdoor life; something that was absent in the United States.

I decided to illustrate books for children because I was concerned about the absence of positive imagery among African American children, a lack that I felt had existed since my own childhood years.

The author and publisher of *Bola and the Oba's Drummers* had seen the work I had done in Africa and felt that my style and the African experience would lend itself to the subject.

The subject matter of *To Be a Slave* is one I feel deeply about as an African American male and as a descendent of African slaves. It was the first book by an African American writer I had had the privilege of illustrating. This added to my desire to express the message Julius Lester was conveying. I feel the resultant work has strong emotional images.

I basically consider myself and my work inseparable. Through my work I express my life and environment, the people and the situation—the truth about things as I see it. The African experience did a great deal to reaffirm my feeling and belief in the beauty and humanism of blacks. My work is one of the greatest satisfactions in my life. My work is my life!

The talent that we possess does not belong to us. It was passed down to us from our ancestors, and they who can best express what our ancestors gave us have the most responsibility to pass this message on to the living and the unborn, so that it can live forever.

Anita Lobel

Anita Lobel was born on June 3, 1934, in Kraków, Poland, and came to the United States at the age of sixteen. While attending the Pratt Institute in Brooklyn, New York, she met Arnold Lobel, who was directing a school play. They soon married. One of the many books she has illustrated, On Market Street *by Arnold Lobel (Greenwillow, 1981), is a Caldecott Honor Book. She lives in New York City.*

I was born into a relatively comfortable merchant family. Hitler put a stop to those comforts. My parents separated for practical reasons, believing we would all have better chances for survival, which proved to be true. My brother, Bernhard, and I were left in the care of a Polish woman, with whom we stayed and drifted around Poland for the next four and a half years. We passed as her children. She was a strong-willed Catholic peasant who saved our lives.

Toward the end of the war my brother and I were captured and sent to a concentration camp, from which we were rescued by Americans on April 15, 1945.

After the war my brother and I were sent to Sweden. We both had tuberculosis and were sent to a sanatorium. It was wonderful! We had food, clean clothes, and were surrounded by nice people.

We were eventually reunited with our parents in Stockholm. I did not go to school until I was thirteen, but was taught how to read and write. I came from Sweden to New York because my parents wanted to renew their relationships with some long-lost relatives they had in this country.

At first I thought only of illustrating stories by other authors. It was Susan Hirschman, a children's book editor at Harper, who inspired me to begin writing children's books. She was my husband's editor and gave him his first job. At that time I was a fabric designer. One Christmas I gave Susan three scarves made from fabrics I had designed. "Why don't you try illustrating children's books?" she asked. I said, "Okay, give me a manuscript, and I'll illustrate it." She said, "No, write it yourself." And that's how it all began. *Sven's Bridge* [Harper, 1965], my first book, developed from a pictorial idea and a character sketch of a kindly man. To my *total* surprise, it was a big success. In 1992 the book was reissued by Greenwillow in a brand-new revised edition.

I feel very strongly that an artist working in the field of children's book illustration should by no means compromise on the graphic design quality of the work. Our senses are bombarded by so much ugliness that it is to be hoped that picture books open a child's eyes and start a future esthetic sense.

The most interesting thing in a book is the space between the pages.

Poets

Poetry is so many things besides the shiver
down the spine.
—David McCord

With a few carefully chosen words, poets transform the ordinary into the extraordinary. Whether their work is serious or hilarious, they bring new life to a myriad of subjects, from asteroids to zinnias. The world of children's literature, as well as the entire world, is enriched by the words of poets.

David McCord

David McCord, born on November 15, 1897, in New York's Green-wich Village, grew up on Long Island, in Princeton, New Jersey, and in Oregon. After graduating from Harvard College in 1921, he published many poems for adults. Far and Few *(1952) was his first book of verse for children. In 1956 he was given the first honorary Doctor of Humane Letters degree from Harvard.* One at a Time: His Collected Poems for the Young *(both Little, Brown) was published in 1977, the same year he became the first recipient of the National Council of Teachers of English Award for Excellence in Poetry for Children. He lives in Boston, Massachusetts.*

I was born at 9 East 10th Street in New York City, but grew up on Long Island. A bad case of malaria when I was three or four years old, recurring at times over several years, and the lack of brothers and sisters turned me toward the world of books and the outdoors.

Long Island was all fields and woods when I was a boy. We lived next door to a poultry farm and not far from the ocean. My love of nature began there. When I was twelve years old, I went with my father and mother to live on a ranch in the south of Oregon on the wild Rogue River. This was frontier country then; no electric lights; oil or coal heat. We pumped all our water out of a deep well. I learned something about birds, animals, and wildflowers, trees and geology, and self-reliance. I learned to weather seasons of drought and weeks of steady rain. I sometimes panned for gold for pocket money. I learned to recognize a few of the constellations and to revere the night sky—Orion is still my favorite skymark! I saw and experienced the terror of a forest fire. I can honestly say that I was a pretty good shot with a rifle, but I haven't aimed at a living thing since I was fifteen. My love of all life is far too deep for that.

Two years after I finished my master's degree in English at Harvard—I had previously studied to become a physicist—I wrote a number of poems for children. One was published in the *Saturday Review of Literature* and got into some anthologies. Soon after that my first book for children, *Far and Few,* appeared.

Sometimes poems come to me full-blown—nonsense verses in particular. More often I work at them, rewriting for choice of words and for sound and smoothness. I never use an unusual word unless I can place it as a key word so that it will make the reader look it up. Poems should open up new horizons. They are vistas—familiar as well as strange.

Children still love words, rhythm, rhyme, music, games. They climb trees, skate, swim, swing, fish, explore, act, ride, run, and love snow and getting wet all over; they make things and are curious about science. They love humor and nonsense and imaginary conversation with imaginary things. I pray I am never guilty of talking down to boys and girls. I try to remember that they are closer to the sixth sense than we who are older.

Poetry, like rain, should fall with elemental music, and poetry for children should catch the eye as well as the ear and the mind. It should delight; it really *has* to delight. Furthermore, poetry for children should keep reminding them, without any feeling on their part that they are being reminded, that the English language is a most marvelous and availing instrument.

Poetry is so many things besides the shiver down the spine. It is a new day lying on a new doorstep. It is what will stir the weariest mind to write. It is the inevitable said so casually that the reader or listener thinks he said it himself. It is the fall of syllables that run as easily as water flowing over a dam. It is fireflies in May, apples in October, the wood fire burning when one looks up from an open book. It is the best dream from which one ever waked too soon. It is *Peer Gynt* and *Moby Dick* in a single line. It is the best translation of words that do not exist. It is hot coffee dripping from an icicle. It is the accident involving sudden life. It is the calculus of the imagination. It is the finishing touch to what one could not finish. It is a hundred things as unexplainable as all our foolish explanations.

Arna Bontemps

Arna Bontemps, born on October 13, 1902, in Alexandria, Louisiana, grew up in California. An active participant in the Harlem Renaissance of the 1920s, he won numerous awards for poems and short stories. In 1932 he collaborated with Langston Hughes to write his first book for children, Popa and Fifina: Children of Haiti *(Macmillan; reissued by Oxford, 1993). His 1937* Sad-Faced Boy *(Houghton) was the first book illustrated by Virginia Lee Burton.* Golden Slippers: An Anthology of Negro Poetry for Children *(Harper), which appeared in 1941, was the first collection of African American poetry for children.* Story of the Negro *(Knopf, 1948) is a Newbery Honor Book. He died on June 4, 1973, in Nashville, Tennessee.*

I wrote *Popo and Fifina* because Langston Hughes had the story and told it to me. But I had the children! So we worked together. Both Langston and Countee Cullen have given me credit for starting them to writing children's books. In his autobiography, *The Big Sea*, Langston wrote in my copy: "For Arna, who prodded me into starting this Big Sea on a train between Toledo and Chicago when we were on a lecture tour. Well, here it is. Thank you! Sincerely, Langston."

I decided to write for young people for two reasons. First, as a child I read a great deal and never forgot the books I had enjoyed most, and secondly, by the time I started writing as a man, I had children of my own and wanted them to read my books—as well as other people's, of course!

When I was compiling *Golden Slippers*, I wrote to Langston Hughes, asking him to send me some poems for the collection. He sent me a large selection, and these lines accompanied them:

> *Dear Arna,*
> > *Some of these are for children,*
> > *And some for older fry,*
> > *You may take your choice,*
> > *Since you're as old as I.*
> > > *Sincerely, Lang.*

Many years after *Golden Slippers* I compiled *Hold Fast to Dreams: Poems Old and New* [Follett, 1969]. Of course the title is from

Langston's most endearing poem, "Dreams." I thought all poems could be divided two ways—the poems we remember and the ones we forget. Mine would be a collection of the poems I remembered well, and some would be old, some new.

What is poetry? The old folks down home used to say when talking about singing or preaching or the old-time religion, "You will shout when it hits you." You may not shout when you remember poems you have read or learned, but you will know from your toes to your head that something—*something*—has hit you.

Aileen Fisher

Aileen Fisher was born on September 9, 1906, in the little town of Iron River, on the Upper Peninsula of Michigan, near the Wisconsin border. Her first book of poetry, The Coffee-Pot Face *(McBride), appeared in 1933. Since then she has written in a wide variety of forms, including plays, biographies, and novels. Best known for her rich body of poetry, she received the 1978 National Council of Teachers of English Award for Excellence in Poetry for Children.* Always Wondering *(Harper, 1991) features eighty of her more popular poems. She lives in Boulder, Colorado.*

When I was four years old, my father had a serious bout with pneumonia that made him decide to retire to the country. He bought forty acres near Iron River and built the big, square, white house where I grew up. We called the place High Banks because it was on a high bank above the river—always red with water pumped from the iron mines. Still, the river was good to wade in, swim in, fish in, and skate on in the winter. When I was young, there was still quite a bit of logging nearby, and my brother and I used to follow the iced logging roads. We had all kinds of pets—cows, horses, and chickens. And we had a big garden each summer. I loved it. I have always loved the country.

I went to the University of Chicago for two years, then transferred to the School of Journalism at the University of Missouri. After receiving my degree in 1927, I worked in a little theater during the summer, then went back to Chicago to look for a job. I found one—an assistant in a placement bureau for women journalists! That fall I sold my first poem, a nine-lined verse entitled "Otherwise," to *Child Life* magazine.

My aim in Chicago was to save every single cent I was able, so I could escape back to the country life I loved and missed. I had to be economical, so I took a cheap, dark, first-floor room in a third-rate hotel on Chicago's South Side. It had only one window, and that opened onto a cement area that led to an alley. Across the panes were bars to keep prowlers away.

The room was furnished with a steel cot, a wardrobe badly in need of varnish, two chairs, and a kitchen table I used as a desk.

Coming in from work one evening, I jotted down nine lines I had thought about on the walk from the station. I then went out to dinner at a small, nearby restaurant where I could get a meal for sixty cents. When I got back to my room, I still liked the nine lines, so I hurriedly sent them off, along with several other verses, to Marjorie Burrows, then editor of *Child Life*.

I continued writing poems for children, and for five years

continued working in Chicago, wondering every single day how I might get back to the country. In 1932 I adamantly decided to get out of the city. I moved and settled in Colorado, where I have lived ever since.

My work habits are quite methodical. I try to be at my desk four hours a day, from eight A.M. to noon. Ideas come to me out of experience and from reading and remembering. I usually do a first draft by hand. I can't imagine writing verse on a machine. I think with a pencil or pen in my hand. I usually re-work my material, sometimes more, sometimes less. I never try out my ideas on children, except on the child I used to know—me!

My pleasures in life are found through animals, especially dogs, mountain climbing, hiking, working with wood, unorthodox gardening, a few people in small doses, and reading. For me early morning on a mountain trail is the height of bliss.

Poetry is a rhythmical piece of writing that leaves the reader feeling that life is a little richer than before, a little more full of wonder, beauty, or just plain delight.

Lilian Moore

Lilian Moore, born on March 17, 1909, in New York City, attended public schools and colleges there. She is the author of many picture books, anthologies, and novels. Her first book of poetry, I Feel the Same Way, *appeared in 1967.* Something New Begins: New and Selected Poems *(1982; both Atheneum) brings together work from six of her earlier volumes. In 1985 she was recipient of the National Council of Teachers of English Award for Excellence in Poetry for Children. She lives in Berkeley, California.*

I can't remember when I didn't in some way think of myself as a writer. One of my earliest memories is of sitting on a big metal box, outside a hardware store on the street where I lived. There was a group of children around me—the friends with whom I went roller-skating and sledding—and there I was telling a series of yarns. I can still remember saying, "To be continued tomorrow." I wrote the plays I put on in the summers, I worked as a camp counselor, and of course, I guess like everyone else, I had half a novel in my drawer that took me years to bring myself to throw out.

While working with youngsters in the New York City schools who needed special help in reading, I began to write for children. I had been identified for a long time with what are called easy-to-read materials, due to my work at the Bureau of Educational Research in New York. I learned from the children the basic difference between dense and open material, but I never understood why people thought that easy-to-read material for children had to be clunky and dull.

Being the editor of Arrow Book Club was one of the most satisfying things I ever did, helping to launch the *first* quality paperback book program for elementary-school children throughout the United States. It was a job that brought together my experience as a teacher, my interest in children's books, my work as a writer, and my downright pleasure in the endearing middle-grader. Imagine making it possible for these youngsters to choose and buy good books for the price of comic books!

I Feel the Same Way was suggested by Jean Karl, my editor at Atheneum. I wrote most of the poems on my way to work. I think of them as my subway songs. Often when I seemed to be staring vacantly at subway ads, I was working intensely on a new idea. As I worked on the poems, I found myself getting in touch with my own memories of childhood and reliving every feeling. Writing this book was so exhilarating that I went on to write more and more poetry.

The grain of sand that's supposed to irritate the creative center and produce a pearl often produces just the irritation. Lines that are supposed to dance drag their iambic feet. Words that are supposed to reflect light remain maddeningly dim. Or a cliché pops up that must be uprooted like a noxious weed. Then it's back to the typewriter, or the ballpoint pen, or a pencil with a good eraser. And another wastebasket to fill.

Poems should be like fireworks, packed carefully and artfully, ready to explode with unpredictable effects.

Beatrice Schenk de Regniers

Beatrice Schenk de Regniers, born August 14, 1914, in Lafayette, Indiana, attended the University of Chicago and Winnetka Graduate Teachers College. Most of her adult life was spent in the field of publishing, working as editor of the Lucky Book Club for Scholastic, Inc. Her first book, The Giant Story, *illustrated by Maurice Sendak (Harper), appeared in 1953.* May I Bring a Friend?, *illustrated by Beni Montresor (Atheneum, 1964), received the Caldecott Award. In addition to picture books, she has written several volumes of poetry for children. She lives in New York City.*

When I was seven, my parents moved to Crawfordsville, Indiana, where I lived a wonderful kind of free childhood, where I could gather violets, live in a tree, walk in the woods—be!

After World War II, I served as educational materials director of the American Heart Association. I got sick of health, so I left!

We had two Siamese-alley cats for ten and eleven years. One of the cats died of cancer; he died in my arms. A year later the other was dying, and I was so distressed, I decided to write to focus on something else. *May I Bring a Friend?* was done in an almost mechanized way. I said, "I'll write and not think of cats. I'll write verse because it demands concentration." I didn't know what I was going to write about, but when the book was finished, oddly enough it was filled with animals—but no cats.

Beni Montresor and I worked closely together on the book. We'd call one another and discuss situations on the phone. I wasn't the least bit surprised that it won the Caldecott Award. I expect all the illustrators of my books to win it. As a matter of fact, three of them—Maurice Sendak, Beni, and Nonny Hogrogian—have!

All of my books have their own way of working themselves out from me, but most of them begin in a meadow. I take my notebook and my pencil and go away, alone, to a place where I can be physically in touch with nature. I wander through the countryside and work in a kind of meadow trance.

I had a difficult time getting away when I worked on my book of poems *Something Special* [Harcourt, 1958], so I got up every morning at 5:30 and worked until 7:30 A.M. The dining-room table was my meadow for this book. You know how still everything is between five and seven. The house is so quiet.

What some people may not know about my books is that a very thin book usually means a very fat wastebasket.

I love to dance. In my reincarnation I'm going to be a choreographer. My writing is a kind of dance. I want all my books to have a pace, a movement, like a ballet.

John Ciardi

John Ciardi was born on June 24, 1916, in Boston, the only son of Italian immigrant parents, and grew up in Medford, Massachusetts. He was one of America's foremost poets and a noted translator of Dante's Divine Comedy. *His first volume of poems for children,* The Reason for the Pelican, *appeared in 1959 (Lippincott); in*

*1994 the 35th Anniversary Edition was published (Boyds Mills).
From 1956 to 1972 he was poetry editor of the* Saturday Review.
*In 1982 he was the recipient of the National Council of Teachers of
English Award for Excellence in Poetry for Children. He died on
March 30, 1986, in Edison, New Jersey.*

From about 1947 to 1953, I wrote poetry for my sister's children, when my wife and I were living with them. Subsequently, I wrote for my own children as they came along, and then for myself. The children were eager to grow up; I wasn't, so I wrote for my own childhood.

I Met a Man [Houghton, 1961] remains my favorite book because I wrote it on a first-grade vocabulary level when my daughter, Myra, was in kindergarten. I wanted it to be the first book she read through, and she learned to read from it.

The Monster Den [Lippincott, 1966] is about my three children. It was a way of spoofing them. Kidding with love and some restraint can be a happy relationship. We were never a somber family. I often write spoofs. I have written some adult poems *about* children that are *not* for them. The closest I come to pointing out the difference between poetry for children and poetry for adults is that children's poems are *eternal;* adult poems are *mortal.*

My work for children is based on the premise that poetry and learning are both fun, and children are full of an enormous relish for both. My poetry is just a bubbling up of a natural foolishness, and the idea that maybe you can make language dance a bit. Being a poet is like being a musician. You get caught up in the music. You're drawn to it. So it is with language. It's an instrument, and you can't stop playing.

What is poetry? Poetry is where every line comes to rest against a white space.

I only hope that my work, or part of my work, could stand the test Emily Dickinson used to ask. She would send her poems to editors, and her question always was, "Have I said it true?" She never said, "Have I said it pretty?" or "Have I said it beautiful?" but "Have I said it true?" I think this is the test. You want a sense of reality in what you are writing. It's terribly easy to deceive yourself. I want to think that I "said it true."

Eve Merriam

Eve Merriam, born on July 19, 1916, in Germantown, a suburb of Philadelphia, Pennsylvania, wrote plays, fiction, nonfiction, and poetry for adults. In 1946 she received the Yale Younger Poets Prize for Family Circle, *her first collection of adult poems. In 1981 she received the National Council of Teachers of English Award for Excellence in Poetry for Children. She died on April 11, 1992, in New York City.* The Singing Green: New and Selected Poems for All Seasons *(1992), a collection of more than fifty out-of-print selections and twelve new works, and* Higgle Wiggle: Happy Rhymes *(1994, both Morrow) were published posthumously.*

While I was a student, I had my poetry published in various school publications. I began studying at Columbia University in New York City for my master's degree, but one day, while taking a walk across the George Washington Bridge, I decided *not* to walk back to Columbia. I quit my studies and decided to find a job. It seemed like a good idea—but what could a poet do? I remembered reading somewhere that Carl Sandburg once worked in advertising, so I would, too. I got a job as an advertising copywriter on Madison Avenue and progressed to become a fashion editor for glamor magazines.

When my first poem was published, it was in a little magazine printed on butcher paper, but it was gold to me.

I find it difficult to sit still when I hear poetry or read it out loud. I feel a stinging all over, particularly in the tips of my fingers and in my toes, and it just seems to go right from my mouth all the way through my body. It's like a shot of adrenaline or oxygen when I hear rhymes and word play. Word play is really central for me. I try to give young people a sense of the sport and the playfulness of language, because I think it's like a game. There is a physical element in reading poetry out loud; it's like jumping rope or throwing a ball. If we can get teachers to read poetry, lots of it, out loud to children, we'll develop a generation of poetry readers; we may even have some poetry writers, but the main thing, we'll have language appreciators.

Writing poetry is trying to get a fresh look at something—all poetry is. It's a matter of seeking out sense memories and trying to recapture the freshness of the first time you've experienced things. A poem is very much like you, and that is quite natural, since there is a rhythm in your own body—in your pulse, in your heartbeat, in the way you breathe, laugh, or cry, in the very way you speak. What can a poem do? Just about everything.

Myra Cohn Livingston

Myra Cohn Livingston, born on August 17, 1926, in Omaha, Nebraska, moved with her family to California at the age of eleven. A student of the French horn, she played with the Los Angeles Philharmonic Orchestra at the age of sixteen. She began writing poetry while a freshman at Sarah Lawrence College in New York. Her first book, Whispers and Other Poems *(Harcourt), appeared in 1958. The author of many volumes of original poems, anthologies, and professional books, she is the recipient of the 1980 National Council of Teachers of English Award for Excellence in Poetry for Children and of the 1994 Kerlan Award. In addition to writing, she teaches creative writing and lectures widely throughout the country.* Poem-Making: Ways to Begin Writing Poetry *appeared in 1991 (Harper). She lives in Beverly Hills, California.*

While a freshman at Sarah Lawrence I turned in some poems that my professor felt were for children. She urged me to submit them to *Story Parade* magazine, and in 1946 "Whispers" became my first published poem. I submitted a complete manuscript, *Whispers and Other Poems,* to several publishing houses; it was rejected. Margaret K. McElderry, who was then a children's book editor at Harcourt, urged me, however, to continue writing. Twelve years later I sent the manuscript back to her at Harcourt; it was accepted and published in 1958.

Whispers and Other Poems tells of the quiet, idyllic sort of childhood world I had in Omaha, Nebraska. I shall probably never lose the curiosity of this childhood, the sense of wonder over the metaphysical universe.

Trained as a traditionalist in poetry, I feel strongly about the importance of order imposed by fixed forms, meter, and rhyme when I write about some things; yet free verse seems more suitable for other subjects. It is the force of what I say that shapes the form.

Poetry comes in strange ways and never at the moment when one might think it should come. There are poems I have tried to write for twenty years that have never come out right. Others seem to come in a flash. Searching for the right form to express certain ideas takes time.

I compile poetry anthologies, stores of poetry written by poets of all ages, all nationalities, to demonstrate that there are eternal truths and values that can never be eradicated, ideals that human beings, from the earliest times, have sought. To learn that Greeks sent valentines in the second century, that the meaning of holidays is different for individuals, that men and women have always joyed and sorrowed in love—this and much more may be found in poetry. Readers will also find in anthologies poems and poets that heighten their own individual sensitivities to language, thought, and feeling.

Poem-Making is the result of more than thirty years of teaching in the Dallas Public Library and in the Dallas and Beverly Hills schools, and conducting public workshops throughout the country both as a teacher and poet. Originally, I did some articles for *Cricket* magazine on the writing of poetry, and spoke to Charlotte Zolotow, my editor at Harper, about the possibility of extending these articles and writing a book that might be of help to young people who wish to write poetry. It took me about four years from its inception to publication.

I think I was spurred on to write this book due to my constant contact with children. I also feel children are given so much misinformation about poetry writing that I wanted to pass on the craft I had learned.

A part of me has grown up and lives in a world of adults. But another part of me still remains in the world of childhood, in a world of curiosity and wonder, touching and seeing for the first time, and dreaming of what lies beyond. This childlike part is visible to others when I write poetry, for it celebrates whatever I see and whatever I wonder. Sometimes it is the excitement over the coming of a season, a flower, the shape of clouds or ocean waves. It may be the joy I feel at holiday time. Poetry is my way of sharing with others the way I look at a world that we can all celebrate together.

Karla Kuskin

Karla Kuskin, born on July 17, 1932, in New York City, grew up in Greenwich Village. While attending the Yale School of Design, where she graduated with a B.F.A. degree in 1955, she wrote and illustrated her first book for children, Roar and More *(1956), as part of a thesis. She has created many different types of books, including books of poetry.* Dogs & Dragons, Trees & Dreams *(1980; both Harper) contains work written between 1958 and 1975. In 1979 she received the National Council of Teachers of English Award for Excellence in Poetry for Children. She lives in Brooklyn, New York, and Arlington, Virginia.*

As far back as I can remember, poetry has had a special place in my life. As a young, only child, I would make up rhymes, which my mother wrote down and read back to me. And my father wrote verse to and for me. As I began to learn to read, I was encouraged by my parents to read aloud. I was also fortunate that in elementary school I had teachers who read poetry aloud and who greatly influenced my love of verse. I guess I grew up with a metronomic beat inside my head, which fortunately never left.

One of the reasons I write for children is to entice some of them into sharing my lifelong enjoyment of reading and writing, as my parents and teachers did when they communicated their own love of words to me. Instead of building a fence of formality around poetry, I want to emphasize its accessibility, the sound, rhythm, humor, the inherent simplicity. Poetry can be as natural and effective a form of self-expression as singing and shouting.

When I write poetry, wherever I look I find I'm thinking in terms of words and rhythms and sound. Lines that might go through my head I try to hang on to. I'm afraid I let a lot of good lines go at times when I'm not receptive. It's being receptive that has a great deal to do with what you write.

The hardest thing in the world is being a critic of your own work. For me time has always been the best critic. If I can put something away and then come back, it's like taking a painting you're working on, turning it upside down, squinting at it, or walking away to get a new view. Time helps you know whether it's worth saving or whether it should be dumped.

Joseph Joubert, a French critic, once said, "You will find poetry nowhere unless you bring some of it with you." To which might be added that if you do bring some of it with you, you will find it everywhere.

Valerie Worth

Valerie Worth, born on October 29, 1933, in Philadelphia, Pennsylvania, grew up in nearby Swarthmore. In 1972 her first book, Small Poems, *was published.* More Small Poems *(1976),* Still More Small Poems *(1978), and* Small Poems Again *(1986) followed.* All the Small Poems, *collected works from the four editions, appeared in paperback in 1987, and* All the Small Poems and Fourteen More *was published in 1994 (all Farrar). In 1991, she received the National Council of Teachers of English Award for Excellence in Poetry for Children. She died on July 31, 1994, at her home in Clinton, New York.*

Although I loved reading poetry as a child, something in me felt unsatisfied, as if something more could be done with it. When I turned to writing, I tried to create what I wanted when I was a child—poetry that would reach more deeply into the world I saw around me.

When my husband began teaching at Kirkland College, I joined an informal writing group, where I met Natalie Babbitt. I read some of my poems aloud to the group. When Natalie heard them, she said, "I'd like to send your poems to Michael di Capua at Farrar, Straus & Giroux to look at." The whole experience was a most fortuitous one. Shortly after my work was sent to Michael di Capua, he offered to publish my first volume, *Small Poems*. This was a great time for me. I had been writing for a long time and wasn't publishing much. I had sent my work around to publishers for several years, and I had no luck at all getting it published. This is a good lesson for young writers—*never* give up if you believe in your work.

I write about what is vivid, exciting, magical to me—about the way I see things now, or how I viewed them as a child—or a combination of both child/adult feelings. I write about things that strike a chord in me, be it a lawn mower or a kaleidoscope or coat hangers. I have strong responses to what find their ways into my work. It has always seemed to me that any tree or flower, any living creature, even any old board or brick or bottle, possesses a mysterious poetry of its own; a poetry still wordless, formless, inaudible, but asking to be translated into words and images and sounds—to be expressed as a poem. Perhaps it could be said that written poetry is simply a way of revealing and celebrating the essentially poetic nature of the world itself.

Some of my poems just spring up—full bloom! Others can take days, weeks, months. Usually ideas come first, then the poetry takes hold. It is a matter of thought, sound, imagery—all working together in balance to create the effect that I want to convey. Then there are times I know I am going in a wrong direction, and I have to pull back—pull back strongly and start all over. My aim is to focus clearly on a subject, pare down words so there can be nothing extraneous in any of my poems. "Water Lily," a verse containing ten lines with a total of twenty words, was one such poem that just wouldn't work. After almost one hundred versions everything fitted into place.

I would tell children who want to write poetry to write poetry for the fun of it, for the joy of it, for the love of it. And especially for the love of the things you write about, whatever they may be—whether beautiful or ugly, grand or humble, birds of paradise or mosquitoes, stars or mud puddles: All are worthy of being written about if you feel a deep affection for them—or, indeed, if you feel strongly about them in any way at all. But never forget that the subject is as important as your feeling: The mud puddle itself is as important as your pleasure in looking at it or splashing through it. Never let the mud puddle get lost in the poetry—because, in many ways, the mud puddle *is* the poetry.

Arnold Adoff

Arnold Adoff was born on July 16, 1935, in the South Bronx, New York City, and taught in public schools in Harlem and on Manhattan's Upper West Side. In 1968 he published his first anthology, I Am the Darker Brother: An Anthology of Modern Poems by Negro Americans *(Macmillan). After compiling additional anthologies, he began writing his own poetry. In 1969 he moved to Yellow Springs, Ohio, where he lives with his wife, the writer Virginia Hamilton. In 1988 Mr. Adoff received the National Council of Teachers of English Award for Excellence in Poetry for Children.*

I grew up in and around the Bronx and all over the city and loved New York and its potential for power, excitement, and discovery. There was too much to see, always too much to read, always another place to go. The neighborhood had character—solid, respectable Jewish middle class: the butcher, the grocer, my father's pharmacy on the corner, the old ladies sitting in the front of the stoops, mothers waiting with jars of milk for the kids to have afternoon snacks after school before running to Crotona Park to play ball. Books and food, recipes and political opinions, Jewish poetry, and whether the dumplings would float on top of the soup were all of equal importance. And reading, of course. I read everything in the house and then all I could carry home each week from the libraries I could reach on Bronx buses.

I began collecting literature for my classes while teaching in the late 1950s and early 1960s. I have been a poet, deep inside, since I began writing as a teenager. By thirty, I was enough of a man to start to put things together and realize where the thrust should be directed. I wanted to influence the kids coming up—I wanted to anthologize adult literature of the highest literary quality and get it into classrooms and libraries for children and young adults. From that time on, I threw myself full force into creating books for children.

I look for craft and control in making a form that is unique to the individual poem, that shapes it, holds it tight, creates an inner tension that makes a whole shape out of the words.

When I am drafting a poem, I visualize myself surfing—only I don't surf, but I'm kind of doing so on a word processor or on a sheet of paper. That's the way kids should be gliding into the process of revision—not sweating and grinding, attempting to find a word that rhymes at the end of a line that could be in any way close to what they *really* wanted to say. Why create more locks? Why create more prisons? Why not open up a few walls?

Jack Prelutsky

Jack Prelutsky was born on September 8, 1940, in Brooklyn, New York, and attended New York City public schools, graduating from the High School of Music and Art, where he studied voice. He began writing verse to fill up his long hours while working in a Greenwich Village music store. At the suggestion of a friend, he showed some of his verses to Susan Hirschman, editor of children's books at Macmillan, who encouraged him to continue writing. In 1967 his first book, A Gopher in the Garden *(Macmillan), appeared. In addition to writing volumes of original verse, including* The New Kid on the Block *(1984) and* Something Big Has Been Here *(1990; both Greenwillow), he has compiled many anthologies for children. He lives near Seattle, Washington.*

There was a time when I simply couldn't stand poetry. In grade school I had a teacher who left me with the impression that poetry was the literary equivalent of liver, something I detest. I was told it was good for me, but I wasn't convinced. When I rediscovered poetry in my twenties, I decided I would write about things that kids really cared about, and that I would make poetry delightful. I think my work appeals to children because I'm in close touch with my own childhood; I have a pretty good idea of what children find funny or what they find scary. Also, I never talk down to them.

Becoming a writer was a wonderful case of serendipity and came as a complete surprise to me. In my early twenties, when I was searching for myself in the manner of many young people, I had a lot of trouble deciding just what it was that I wanted to do with my life. Although I had a strong suspicion that I was meant to be an artist, I didn't know what kind. I began experimenting with a variety of disciplines—photography, folk music, classical singing, sculpture, collage.

One evening a close friend of mine accidentally noticed a bunch of verses on my desk and urged me to show them to his editor. She hated the drawings I did for the verses, but I had at last found my medium—writing.

One day I bought some boneless breast of chicken at a local market, and I started wondering if the rest of the chicken was boneless, too. This let me to write a poem entitled "Ballad of a Boneless Chicken," which is in *The New Kid on the Block*. Incidentally, she lays scrambled eggs!

I find it impossible not to have ideas. For me, having ideas is as natural a function as breathing. As long as I keep my senses alert and remain open to the world, the ideas continue to flow. They are everywhere, in everything I see, read, feel, smell, taste, and touch. Dreams and memories are wonderful sources. One of the great joys in having this procession of ideas is that I am never bored.

Appendix: Major Awards

The listings below cite the name of each author and illustrator who appears in this volume.

Hans Christian Andersen Award _____

The most distinguished prize in children's literature, this award is given biennially by the International Board on Books for Young People, to authors since 1956 and illustrators since 1966, for lasting contributions to literature for children. The United States medalists include:

> 1962—Meindert DeJong
> 1970—Maurice Sendak
> 1972—Scott O'Dell
> 1992—Virginia Hamilton

Randolph J. Caldecott Award _____

The Caldecott Award, named after the outstanding nineteenth-century English illustrator Randolph Caldecott, has been given annually since 1938 by the American Library Association. It is awarded "to the artist of the most distinguished American picture book for children published in the United States during the preceding year." In addition to the winner, an unspecified number of Honor Books are named each year. Honor Books by illustrators who appear in this volume are noted in the biographical introductions. The following are the illustrators in this volume who were awarded the Caldecott Medal, and the years in which they received their awards.

1938—Dorothy P. Lathrop
1940—Edgar Parin and Ingri d'Aulaire
1942—Robert McCloskey
1944—Louis Slobodkin
1947—Leonard Weisgard
1948—Roger Duvoisin
1949—Berta and Elmer Hader
1950—Leo Politi
1952—Nicolas Mordvinoff
1953—Lynd Ward
1955—Marcia Brown
1956—Feodor Rojankovsky
1957—Marc Simont
1958—Robert McCloskey
1960—Marie Hall Ets
1962—Marcia Brown
1963—Ezra Jack Keats
1964—Maurice Sendak
1965—Beni Montresor
1966—Nonny Hogrogian
1967—Evaline Ness
1968—Ed Emberley
1969—Uri Shulevitz
1972—Nonny Hogrogian
1973—Blair Lent
1978—Peter Spier
1981—Arnold Lobel
1983—Marcia Brown

Lee Bennett Hopkins Poetry Award

Established in 1993, this award is presented annually by the Children's Literature Council of Pennsylvania to a living American poet or compiler for the most distinguished volume of poetry published during the preceding year.

>   1993—Ashley Bryan

Kerlan Award

The Kerlan Award, given by the Kerlan Collection of the University of Minnesota Libraries in Minneapolis, Minnesota, has been presented annually since 1975 "in recognition of singular attainments in the creation of children's literature and in appreciation for generous donations of unique resources to the Kerlan Collection for the study of children's literature."

>   1975—Elizabeth Coatsworth
>   Marie Hall Ets
>   1976—Roger Duvoisin
>   1978—Carol Ryrie Brink
>   1981—Tomie dePaola
>   1982—Jean Craighead George
>   1986—Charlotte Zolotow
>   1990—Madeleine L'Engle
>   1993—Mary Stolz
>   1994—Myra Cohn Livingston

Coretta Scott King Award

Presented annually by the Coretta Scott King Task Force of the American Library Association's Social Responsibilites Round Table, this Award honors African American authors and illustrators whose distinguished books promote an understanding and appreciation of the culture and contribution of all people to the realization of the "American dream." The Award commemorates the life and work of Dr. Martin Luther King, Jr., and honors his widow, Coretta Scott King, for her courage and determination in continuing the work for peace and world brotherhood.

The Award was founded in 1969 by the late Glyndon Flynt Greer, a distinguished school librarian. The Award became an official ALA unit Award in 1982.

>   1979—Tom Feelings
>   1981—Ashley Bryan
>   1983—Virginia Hamilton
>   1986—Virginia Hamilton
>   1994—Tom Feelings

National Council of Teachers of English Award for Excellence in Poetry for Children

First presented in 1977, this award was given annually to a living American poet for an aggregate body of work. Since 1982, the award has been given every three years.

>   1977—David McCord
>   1978—Aileen Fisher
>   1979—Karla Kuskin

1980—Myra Cohn Livingston
1981—Eve Merriam
1982—John Ciardi
1985—Lilian Moore
1988—Arnold Adoff
1991—Valerie Worth

John Newbery Award

Awarded annually since 1922, the Newbery Award, named after John Newbery, an eighteenth-century English publisher and bookseller, is presented to an American "author of the most distinguished contribution to American literature for children published in the U.S. during the preceding year." In addition to the winner, an unspecified number of Honor Books are also cited. Honor Books by authors who appear in this volume are noted in the biographical introductions. The following are the authors in this volume who were awarded the Newbery Medal, and the years in which they received their awards.

1931—Elizabeth Coatsworth
1936—Carol Ryrie Brink
1940—James Daugherty
1946—Lois Lenski
1950—Marguerite de Angeli
1951—Elizabeth Yates
1952—Eleanor Estes
1955—Meindert DeJong
1956—Jean Lee Latham
1957—Virginia Sorensen
1958—Harold Keith

1959—Elizabeth George Speare
1961—Scott O'Dell
1962—Elizabeth George Speare
1963—Madeleine L'Engle
1966—Elizabeth Borten de Treviño
1967—Irene Hunt
1968—E. L. Konigsburg
1969—Lloyd Alexander
1970—William Armstrong
1971—Betsy Byars
1973—Jean Craighead George
1975—Virginia Hamilton
1979—Ellen Raskin
1984—Beverly Cleary
1985—Robin McKinley

Regina Medal

Established in 1959 by the Catholic Library Association, the Regina Medal is given to a living author "to dramatize the timeless standards and ideals for the writing of good literature for children."

1966—Leo Politi
1968—Marguerite de Angeli
1969—Lois Lenski
1970—Edgar Parin and Ingri d'Aulaire
1972—Meindert DeJong
1974—Robert McCloskey
1975—Lynd Ward
1977—Marcia Brown

1978—Scott O'Dell
1980—Beverly Cleary
1982—Dr. Seuss
1983—Tomie dePaola
1984—Madeleine L'Engle
1985—Jean Fritz
1986—Lloyd Alexander
1987—Betsy Byars
1990—Virginia Hamilton

University of Southern Mississippi Medallion

Established in 1969, this annual award honors an author or illustrator whose body of work has made an outstanding contribution to the field of children's literature.

1969—Lois Lenski
1971—Roger Duvoisin
1972—Marcia Brown
1973—Lynd Ward
1974—Taro Yashima
1976—Scott O'Dell
1978—Madeleine L'Engle
1980—Ezra Jack Keats
1981—Maurice Sendak
1982—Beverly Cleary
1984—Peter Spier
1985—Arnold Lobel
1986—Jean Craighead George
1988—Jean Fritz
1990—Charlotte Zolotow

1994—Ashley Bryan
1995—Tomie dePaola

Laura Ingalls Wilder Award ━━━━━━━━━━━━━━━━━━

Named for the creator of the Little House series, this award, sponsored by the Association for Library Services for Children, a division of the American Library Association, is presented to an American author or illustrator whose books have made a substantial and lasting contribution to children's literature. Established in 1954, the award was given every five years from 1960 to 1980. From 1983 to the present, it has been awarded every three years.

1970—E. B. White
1975—Beverly Cleary
1980—Dr. Seuss
1983—Maurice Sendak
1986—Jean Fritz
1989—Elizabeth George Speare
1992—Marcia Brown
1995—Virginia Hamilton

Index

Lee Bennett Hopkins writes and lectures frequently on teaching poetry to children. The founder of two poetry awards, Mr. Hopkins has close to one hundred books to his credit, including two professional titles, *Pass the Poetry, Please!*, which was hailed by ALA *Booklist* as "an inspirational source" for those working at bringing children and poety together, and *Let Them Be Themselves.*

Mr. Hopkins is the winner of the University of Southern Mississippi 1989 Medallion for his distinguished contribution to children's literature. He graduated from Kean College and the Bank Street College of Education and holds a professional diploma in educational supervision and administration from Hunter College. Mr. Hopkins lives in Scarborough, New York.